SOCIAL MEDIA

MEDIA

FOR
REAL
ESTATE
AGENTS

SOCIAL MEDIA

FOR REAL ESTATE AGENTS

Grow your real estate brand and your business
through powerful social media platforms.

CELESTE BELLWOOD

ISBN: 979-8-9882309-3-9 (Print)

Published by Celeste Bellwood. Celeste Bellwood's titles may be purchased in bulk for educational, business, fundraising, or sales promotional use. For information, please email hello@celestebellwood.com

First print edition: 2023

Celeste Bellwood

Unlock the potential of social media to transform your real estate career with this comprehensive guide, covering everything from platform mastery to advanced strategies and tools. Learn to build a powerful online presence, create engaging content, and optimize your digital marketing efforts to generate leads and grow your business.

Dedicated to the incredible real estate agents that keep our industry alive and work hard for their clients every day.

TABLE OF CONTENTS

TABLE OF CONTENTS CONT.

TABLE OF CONTENTS CONT.

TABLE OF CONTENTS CONT.

INTRODUCTION

In recent years, the real estate industry has experienced a significant paradigm shift, fueled by rapid advancements in technology and the ever-evolving digital landscape. As a result, social media platforms have emerged as essential tools for real estate agents who wish to thrive in an increasingly competitive market. The traditional methods of marketing, such as newspaper ads, direct mail campaigns, and billboards, are no longer sufficient to capture the attention of potential clients. Instead, real estate agents must master the art of utilizing social media platforms to build their brand, grow their business, and generate leads.

This comprehensive book is designed to equip you, as a real estate agent, with the knowledge, strategies, and tactics necessary to harness the power of Facebook, YouTube, Pinterest, TikTok, and Instagram to take your real estate career to new heights.

We will explore the unique characteristics and benefits of each platform, empowering you to craft a social media strategy that resonates with your target audience and translates into tangible results for your business.

In the opening chapters of this book, we will lay the groundwork for understanding the role of social media in today's real estate landscape. We will discuss the benefits of leveraging these platforms and how to establish a strong online presence that sets you apart from the competition. We will also explore the essential elements of creating a cohesive and compelling brand identity across all social media platforms, including setting objectives, defining your target audience, crafting a unique brand voice, and developing a consistent visual identity.

Next, we will delve into the intricacies of each social media platform, starting with Facebook. As the most popular social media platform, Facebook offers immense potential for real estate agents to connect with their audience. We will provide an in-depth look at Facebook marketing strategies, from setting up a professional page and optimizing your profile, to creating engaging content, leveraging Facebook ads, and utilizing Facebook groups and events.

Following our exploration of Facebook, we will turn our attention to YouTube, focusing on the world of video marketing. We will discuss channel creation, video production best practices, optimization techniques, and promotional strategies to maximize your reach. YouTube offers a unique opportunity for real estate agents to showcase properties, share valuable insights, and build a loyal following.

As we continue our journey through the various social media platforms, we will investigate Pinterest's potential for real estate agents. This visual platform can be highly effective in showcasing properties and inspiring potential buyers. We will explore how to create captivating pins, organize boards, collaborate with other users, and utilize Pinterest's advertising options to drive traffic and generate leads.

Subsequently, we will delve into the rapidly growing world of TikTok. This platform has taken the world by storm, and real estate agents can capitalize on its popularity to create entertaining and educational content that appeals to a younger audience. We will cover the basics of using TikTok, including setting up a profile, creating and editing videos, leveraging popular trends, and engaging with the TikTok community.

The next social media platform we will examine is Instagram. As a visual powerhouse, Instagram is perfect for showcasing stunning properties and giving potential clients a glimpse into your daily life as a real estate agent. We will discuss how to optimize your profile, create compelling content, utilize Instagram Stories and IGTV, and engage with your audience to build a strong following.

In addition to providing in-depth analyses of each platform, this book will discuss the importance of integrating your social media efforts across all platforms. We will outline strategies for cross-promotion, content repurposing, and streamlining your workflow. We will also explore the world of social media advertising, focusing on Facebook, Instagram, Pinterest, and YouTube, and discuss targeting options, ad formats, budgeting, and best practices for creating high-converting ads.

To ensure your social media efforts are yielding the desired results, it is crucial to monitor and analyze your performance. We will dedicate a chapter to discussing the key metrics to track, the tools available for social media analytics, and how to interpret data to optimize your strategy and maximize your return on investment. A strong online reputation is critical for real estate agents, as potential clients often rely on reviews and recommendations when choosing an agent. Therefore, we will explore strategies for managing your online reputation, including monitoring reviews, handling negative feedback, and encouraging satisfied clients to share their positive experiences.

As technology and social media platforms continue to evolve, it is essential for real estate agents to stay ahead of the curve. We will dedicate a chapter to discussing emerging trends, new platforms, and potential opportunities for real estate agents to leverage in their social media strategies. Furthermore, we will explore the growing importance of live streaming and virtual reality in the real estate industry and discuss how agents can embrace these technologies to enhance their social media presence.

To ensure that you have a well-rounded understanding of the role of social media in real estate, we will also delve into the legal and ethical considerations surrounding social media usage. This includes discussing the importance of copyright and intellectual property, as well as outlining best practices for ensuring compliance with industry regulations and maintaining client confidentiality.

By the end of this book, you will have gained a comprehensive understanding of the power and potential of social media platforms in the real estate industry.

With this knowledge, you will be well-equipped to create a powerful and effective social media strategy that will set you apart from the competition, attract potential clients, and ultimately, drive the success of your real estate business.

As you embark on this exciting journey, it is important to remember that social media success does not happen overnight. It requires consistent effort, experimentation, and adaptation to the ever-changing landscape of digital marketing. However, with determination, perseverance, and the insights gained from this book, you will be well on your way to harnessing the power of social media to transform your real estate career and achieve the results you desire. So, buckle up and get ready to embark on an exciting journey to social media success in the world of real estate.

Happy selling!

CHAPTER 2:

THE ROLE OF SOCIAL MEDIA IN TODAY'S REAL ESTATE LANDSCAPE

The Evolution of the Real Estate Industry

The real estate industry has experienced a dramatic transformation over the past few decades, with the advent of the internet and the rapid rise of digital technology. Gone are the days when prospective buyers and sellers primarily relied on print advertisements, yard signs, and word-of-mouth referrals to find or sell properties. Today, a vast majority of real estate transactions begin with online searches, and digital marketing has become an indispensable tool for real estate professionals looking to establish a strong presence in the market.

One of the most significant changes in the real estate landscape has been the emergence of social media as a powerful marketing tool.

Social media platforms such as Facebook, Instagram, LinkedIn, Pinterest, Twitter, and TikTok have revolutionized the way real estate agents connect with their audience, promote properties, and build lasting relationships with clients. In this chapter, we will explore the role of social media in today's real estate landscape, and how embracing these platforms can help real estate agents thrive in an increasingly competitive market.

Benefits of Social Media for Real Estate Agents

Social media offers a myriad of benefits for real estate professionals. Here are some of the most compelling advantages of incorporating social media into your marketing strategy:

- Increased visibility: Social media allows real estate agents to reach a wider audience and increase their visibility, both locally and globally. By maintaining a strong presence on popular platforms, agents can tap into vast networks of potential clients, showcase their properties, and generate interest in their services.
- Cost-effective marketing: Traditional marketing channels, such as print advertising, billboards, and direct mail campaigns, can be expensive and time-consuming. Social media, on the other hand, offers an affordable and efficient way to promote your brand, reach your target audience, and stay top-of-mind among potential clients.
- Enhanced communication: Social media facilitates real-time communication and interaction with your audience, allowing you to answer questions,

address concerns, and provide valuable insights into the buying and selling process. This level of engagement fosters trust and credibility, which are essential for building long-lasting relationships with clients.

- Targeted marketing: Social media platforms provide advanced targeting options, enabling real estate agents to deliver their messages to a specific audience based on factors such as demographics, location, interests, and online behavior. This level of precision ensures that your marketing efforts resonate with the right people, maximizing your chances of generating leads and attracting potential clients.
- Networking and collaboration: Social media platforms provide an excellent opportunity for real estate agents to connect with industry professionals, such as mortgage brokers, home inspectors, and interior designers. By fostering these relationships, agents can expand their network, collaborate on projects, and offer a more comprehensive service to their clients.
- Building a personal brand: Social media platforms offer real estate agents an opportunity to showcase their personality, expertise, and values, helping them stand out from the competition and attract clients who resonate with their unique brand identity.

Establishing a Strong Online Presence

To harness the power of social media in today's real estate landscape, it is crucial for agents to establish a strong online presence across multiple platforms.

The following steps outline the process of building a robust and cohesive online presence:

- Choose the right platforms: While it can be tempting to create accounts on every social media platform available, it's essential to focus your efforts on those that are most relevant to your target audience and business objectives. Research each platform's user demographics, engagement patterns, and content formats to determine which ones align best with your goals and resources.
- Optimize your profiles: A well-crafted social media profile serves as a virtual business card, reflecting your brand identity and professionalism. Ensure that your profiles across all platforms are consistent, with a high-quality profile picture, an engaging cover photo, and a succinct yet informative bio. Include relevant keywords, contact information, and links to your website and other online profiles to make it easy for potential clients to find and connect with you.
- Develop a content strategy: Your social media content should be relevant, engaging, and tailored to each platform's unique features and audience preferences. Develop a content strategy that includes a mix of property listings, market updates, industry news, and behind-the-scenes insights into your day-to-day activities as a real estate agent. Aim to strike a balance between promotional and educational content, and don't forget to incorporate visuals, such as high-quality images and videos, to make your posts more engaging.

- Establish a posting schedule: Consistency is key when it comes to building and maintaining a strong online presence. Create a posting schedule that outlines the frequency and timing of your social media updates, taking into account your target audience's online habits and the specific requirements of each platform. Use scheduling tools to automate your posts and ensure that you remain active and visible on social media even during busy periods.
- Engage with your audience: One of the main advantages of social media is the ability to interact directly with your audience, building rapport and trust over time. Respond promptly to comments and messages, and proactively engage with your followers by asking questions, sharing user-generated content, and participating in relevant online discussions. By fostering a sense of community and providing value through your interactions, you can cultivate loyal clients and brand advocates.
- Monitor and analyze performance: To ensure the ongoing success of your social media efforts, it's essential to regularly monitor and analyze your performance. Track key metrics, such as engagement, reach, and conversions, to assess the effectiveness of your content and identify areas for improvement. Make data-driven decisions to refine your strategy, and stay up to date with the latest social media trends and best practices to maintain a competitive edge in the ever-evolving digital landscape.

In conclusion, social media has become an indispensable tool for real estate agents seeking to navigate today's dynamic market.

By establishing a strong online presence, developing a targeted content strategy, and engaging meaningfully with your audience, you can leverage the power of social media to build your brand, generate leads, and ultimately grow your business. As the real estate landscape continues to evolve, staying abreast of emerging trends and adapting your approach to social media marketing will be essential for maintaining a competitive edge and achieving long-term success.

CHAPTER 3:

EVOLUTION OF THE REAL ESTATE INDUSTRY

From Traditional to Digital

The real estate industry has come a long way from its traditional roots, evolving into a complex, technology-driven sector that continues to adapt to shifting consumer behaviors and preferences. In this chapter, we will explore the various factors and innovations that have shaped the industry's evolution and laid the groundwork for the current digital landscape.

- The Pre-Internet Era: Prior to the advent of the internet, the real estate industry relied heavily on print advertising, yard signs, and direct mailing campaigns to promote properties. Real estate agents primarily functioned as gatekeepers of property information, with buyers and sellers depending on their expertise and connections to navigate the market. Networking and word-of-mouth referrals were the primary means of building a client base and securing new business.

- The Rise of the Internet: The introduction of the internet in the 1990s marked a significant turning point for the real estate industry, as property listings and information became increasingly accessible to the general public. Websites such as Realtor.com and Zillow emerged as popular online destinations for buyers and sellers, democratizing access to market data and allowing consumers to conduct their own research and compare properties with ease.

The Emergence of Social Media

The early 2000s saw the birth of social media platforms like MySpace, Facebook, and LinkedIn, which revolutionized the way individuals and businesses connected and communicated online. Over time, social media has become an integral component of the real estate industry, with agents harnessing the power of these platforms to promote their services, showcase properties, and build relationships with clients. The rise of visually driven platforms like Instagram and Pinterest has further emphasized the importance of high-quality images and videos in capturing the attention of potential buyers and sellers.

Technological Innovations Transforming the Industry

The ongoing evolution of the real estate industry can be attributed to several groundbreaking technological innovations that have emerged in recent years:

- Mobile Technology: The widespread adoption of smartphones and mobile devices has had a profound impact on the industry, as buyers and sellers increasingly turn to mobile apps and responsive websites to access real estate information on-the-go. This shift towards mobile browsing has led to a greater emphasis on mobile friendly design and the development of specialized real estate apps that cater to the unique needs of consumers.
- Virtual Reality (VR) and Augmented Reality (AR): VR and AR technologies have opened up new possibilities for property tours and presentations, enabling buyers to virtually explore properties without leaving their homes. This immersive experience not only saves time and resources but also allows agents to showcase properties to a global audience, expanding their reach and potential client base.
- Big Data and Analytics: The emergence of big data and advanced analytics tools has enabled real estate professionals to access and analyze vast amounts of market information, making more informed decisions and developing targeted marketing strategies. This data-driven approach has also led to the rise of predictive analytics and machine learning algorithms, which can help agents identify trends, anticipate market fluctuations, and uncover valuable insights to guide their business strategies.
- Artificial Intelligence (AI) and Chatbots: AI-powered chatbots and virtual assistants have become increasingly popular in the real estate industry, providing instant customer support and answering common queries from potential clients.

These tools can streamline the communication process, allowing agents to focus on more complex tasks and fostering a more personalized, efficient customer experience.

The Future of the Real Estate Industry

As the real estate industry continues to evolve, agents must stay abreast of emerging trends and adapt their approach to remain competitive in the digital landscape. Some key areas to watch in the coming years include:

- The Integration of Smart Home Technology: With the growing popularity of smart home devices and the Internet of Things (IoT), real estate professionals will need to become well-versed in the latest smart home technology and its potential impact on property value and buyer preferences. Agents who can effectively communicate the benefits of smart home features and assist clients in navigating the rapidly changing landscape of home automation will have a competitive edge in the market.
- The Expansion of PropTech: Property technology, or PropTech, refers to the use of technology to streamline and optimize various aspects of the real estate industry, from property management and investment to leasing and sales. As PropTech continues to grow and evolve, real estate professionals will need to embrace new tools and platforms to stay ahead of the curve and better serve their clients.
- The Role of Blockchain and Cryptocurrency: Blockchain technology and cryptocurrency have the potential to revolutionize the real estate industry,

particularly in areas such as property transactions, smart contracts, and title management. While still in its early stages, agents who familiarize themselves with these emerging technologies and their potential applications in the industry will be well-positioned to adapt and thrive as the market evolves.

- Sustainable and Eco-Friendly Practices: As concerns about climate change and environmental sustainability continue to grow, there is an increasing demand for eco-friendly properties and green building practices. Real estate agents who can demonstrate expertise in this area and help clients find properties that align with their environmental values will be in high demand.
- Remote Work and Changing Housing Needs: The COVID-19 pandemic has led to a significant shift in work-from-home culture, with many companies adopting remote work policies and employees seeking more flexible living arrangements. As a result, there is a growing demand for properties with dedicated home office spaces, high-speed internet access, and proximity to outdoor amenities. Real estate agents who can anticipate these changing needs and adapt their services accordingly will be better equipped to serve the needs of the modern buyer.

In conclusion, the real estate industry has undergone a dramatic transformation in recent years, driven by technological innovations and shifting consumer preferences. As the industry continues to evolve, real estate agents must stay informed of emerging trends and technologies, adapting their approach and marketing strategies to remain competitive in an increasingly digital world. By embracing new tools, platforms, and practices, real estate professionals can position themselves for success in the ever-changing landscape of the industry.

CHAPTER 4:

BENEFITS OF SOCIAL MEDIA FOR REAL ESTATE AGENTS

In today's digital age, social media has become an indispensable tool for real estate professionals looking to expand their reach, build brand awareness, and foster relationships with clients. By leveraging popular platforms such as Facebook, Instagram, LinkedIn, Pinterest, Twitter, and TikTok, real estate agents can harness the power of social media to generate leads, showcase properties, and ultimately grow their business. In this chapter, we will delve into the numerous benefits of incorporating social media into your marketing strategy and discuss how these platforms can help you achieve success in the real estate industry.

Expanding Your Reach and Visibility

One of the most significant benefits of using social media for real estate marketing is the ability to reach a wide audience and increase your visibility, both locally and globally.

With millions of users logging onto social media platforms daily, maintaining a strong presence on these networks can help you tap into vast pools of potential clients and generate interest in your properties and services. By consistently sharing valuable content and engaging with your audience, you can establish yourself as a trusted expert in your local market and attract new business through organic reach and word-of-mouth referrals.

Cost-Effective Marketing

Traditional marketing channels, such as print advertising, billboards, and direct mail campaigns, can be costly and time-consuming, often yielding limited results. Social media, on the other hand, offers a more affordable and efficient way to promote your brand, showcase your properties, and engage with your target audience. By utilizing the various features and tools available on social media platforms, such as sponsored posts, targeted ads, and hashtags, you can optimize your marketing efforts to maximize your return on investment and reach the right people at the right time.

Enhanced Communication and Engagement

Social media facilitates real-time communication and interaction with your audience, allowing you to answer questions, address concerns, and provide valuable insights into the buying and selling process. This level of engagement fosters trust and credibility, which are essential for building long-lasting relationships with clients.

By actively participating in online discussions and responding to comments and messages, you can demonstrate your commitment to customer service, showcase your expertise, and cultivate a loyal following.

Targeted Marketing and Personalization

One of the key advantages of social media marketing is the ability to deliver personalized content to a specific audience based on factors such as demographics, location, interests, and online behavior. Advanced targeting options available on social media platforms enable real estate agents to hone in on their ideal client profiles and ensure that their marketing efforts resonate with the right people. By tailoring your content and messaging to the unique needs and preferences of your target audience, you can increase the likelihood of generating leads and attracting potential clients.

Networking and Collaboration

Social media platforms provide an excellent opportunity for real estate agents to connect with industry professionals, such as mortgage brokers, home inspectors, interior designers, and fellow agents. By fostering these relationships and actively participating in relevant online communities and groups, you can expand your network, share ideas, collaborate on projects, and offer a more comprehensive service to your clients. In addition, establishing a strong online presence can help you attract valuable partnerships and referral opportunities, further bolstering your reputation and success in the industry.

Building a Personal Brand

In the competitive world of real estate, developing a unique and authentic personal brand is crucial for setting yourself apart from your competitors and attracting clients who resonate with your values and approach. Social media platforms offer an unparalleled opportunity to showcase your personality, expertise, and style, allowing you to connect with your audience on a deeper level and establish a memorable brand identity. By sharing engaging content that reflects your voice and values, you can cultivate a loyal following and build a strong reputation as a trusted real estate professional in your market.

Analytics and Performance Tracking

Social media platforms offer a wealth of data and analytics tools that enable real estate agents to track the performance of their marketing efforts and make data-driven decisions to refine their strategy. By monitoring key metrics, such as engagement, reach, conversions, and click-through rates, you can identify what types of content resonate with your audience and optimize your approach accordingly. This continuous process of analysis and improvement ensures that your social media marketing efforts remain effective and aligned with your business goals.

Staying Abreast of Industry Trends and News

In the fast-paced world of real estate, staying up-to-date with the latest industry trends, news, and regulations is essential for maintaining a competitive edge and providing informed advice to your clients. Social media platforms serve as valuable sources of real-time information, allowing you to follow industry influencers, participate in online discussions, and share relevant updates with your audience. By staying informed and actively engaging in industry-related conversations, you can position yourself as a knowledgeable and reliable resource for your clients.

Showcasing Properties with Visual Content

The visual nature of social media platforms, particularly Instagram, Pinterest, and TikTok, makes them ideally suited for showcasing properties and highlighting their unique features. High-quality images, videos, and virtual tours can bring a property to life, allowing potential buyers to explore a space and visualize themselves living there. By incorporating visually appealing content into your social media marketing strategy, you can generate interest in your listings and attract more prospective clients.

In conclusion, the benefits of utilizing social media for real estate marketing are numerous and varied.

From expanding your reach and visibility to enhancing communication and engagement, social media platforms offer a powerful and cost-effective way to promote your brand, showcase properties, and generate leads. By developing a targeted and authentic social media presence, real estate agents can capitalize on the many opportunities presented by these platforms and achieve greater success in today's competitive real estate landscape.

CHAPTER 5:

ESTABLISHING A STRONG ONLINE PRESENCE

A strong online presence is crucial for real estate agents looking to succeed in today's competitive market. With the majority of property searches now beginning online and an increasing number of clients relying on social media to find and research potential agents, it is more important than ever to establish a robust digital footprint that showcases your expertise, values, and unique selling proposition. In this chapter, we will discuss the key steps involved in building a powerful online presence, including creating an engaging website, optimizing your social media profiles, and developing a cohesive content strategy.

Creating a Professional Website

Your website serves as the foundation of your online presence and is often the first point of contact for potential clients. To make a strong first impression, it is essential to create a professional, user-friendly, and visually appealing website that showcases your services, expertise, and property listings.

Key elements to consider when designing your website include:

1. Responsive Design: Ensure that your website is mobile-friendly and adapts seamlessly to different screen sizes and devices. With the majority of users now browsing the web on their smartphones, a responsive design is essential for providing a positive user experience and retaining potential clients.
2. User-Friendly Navigation: Make it easy for visitors to find the information they are looking for by organizing your content into clear categories and providing intuitive navigation menus.
3. High-Quality Images and Videos: Incorporate eye-catching visuals that showcase your properties, including high-resolution images, video walkthroughs, and virtual tours. This not only enhances the aesthetic appeal of your website but also helps potential clients better understand the features and benefits of the properties you are marketing.
4. Client Testimonials and Reviews: Showcase your expertise and build trust by featuring positive client testimonials and reviews on your website. This social proof can help reassure potential clients of your professionalism and commitment to customer satisfaction.
5. Search Engine Optimization (SEO): Implement SEO best practices to improve your website's visibility in search engine results and attract more organic traffic. This includes optimizing your site's metadata, using relevant keywords, and creating high-quality, engaging content that provides value to your target audience.

Optimizing Your Social Media Profiles

Your social media profiles serve as an extension of your brand and play a critical role in building your online presence. To maximize the effectiveness of your social media efforts, it is essential to optimize your profiles on all major platforms, including Facebook, Instagram, LinkedIn, Twitter, Pinterest, and TikTok. Key steps to consider when optimizing your profiles include:

1. Consistent Branding: Ensure that your branding elements, such as your logo, colors, fonts, and imagery, are consistent across all your social media profiles. This helps create a cohesive and memorable brand identity that resonates with your audience.
2. Complete and Accurate Information: Provide detailed and up-to-date information on your profiles, including your contact information, website, and a brief description of your services and expertise. This not only helps potential clients find and connect with you but also improves your profiles' visibility and credibility.
3. Customized Cover and Profile Images: Use professional, high-quality images for your profile and cover photos that align with your branding and showcase your personality. This helps create a strong visual impression and attracts the attention of potential clients.
4. Call-to-Action: Include a clear call-to-action on your profiles, encouraging users to visit your website, get in touch, or sign up for your newsletter. This helps drive traffic to your website and generates leads for your business.

Developing a Cohesive Content Strategy

A well-rounded content strategy is essential for maintaining an active and engaging online presence. By sharing valuable, informative, and entertaining content across your website and social media profiles, you can establish yourself as an industry expert, attract and retain potential clients, and foster long-lasting relationships. Key components of a successful content strategy include:

- Content Planning: Develop a content calendar that outlines your posting schedule, content themes, and marketing objectives. This helps ensure that your content remains consistent, relevant, and aligned with your overall marketing strategy.
- Diverse Content Formats: Leverage various content formats, such as blog posts, images, videos, infographics, and live streams, to keep your audience engaged and cater to different preferences and learning styles.
- Educational Content: Provide valuable insights and information about the real estate industry, such as market updates, home buying or selling tips, and local community highlights. This not only positions you as a knowledgeable resource but also helps build trust with your audience.
- Storytelling and Personalization: Share personal stories, anecdotes, and behind-the-scenes glimpses into your daily life as a real estate agent. This helps humanize your brand and fosters a deeper connection with your audience.

- User-Generated Content: Encourage clients to share their experiences working with you, such as testimonials, images of their new homes, or success stories. This not only provides social proof but also helps create a sense of community and loyalty among your clients.
- Consistent Engagement: Actively engage with your audience by responding to comments, answering questions, and participating in relevant online discussions. This not only helps build rapport but also demonstrates your commitment to customer service and support.
- Performance Analysis: Regularly assess the performance of your content by tracking key metrics, such as engagement, reach, and conversions. Use these insights to refine your content strategy and ensure that your efforts continue to deliver results.

Leveraging Online Advertising

In addition to organic content and engagement, online advertising can be a powerful tool for boosting your online presence and generating leads. Platforms such as Facebook, Instagram, and LinkedIn offer targeted advertising options that enable you to reach your ideal audience based on factors such as demographics, location, interests, and online behavior. By allocating a portion of your marketing budget to online advertising, you can amplify your reach, increase your visibility, and drive more traffic to your website and social media profiles.

Establishing a strong online presence is essential for real estate agents looking to thrive in today's digital landscape. By creating a professional website, optimizing your social media profiles, developing a cohesive content strategy, and leveraging online advertising, you can effectively showcase your expertise, build your brand, and attract new clients. As the real estate industry continues to evolve, maintaining a robust online presence will remain a critical component of your overall marketing strategy and long-term success.

CHAPTER 6:

BUILDING YOUR REAL ESTATE BRAND ON SOCIAL MEDIA

In the competitive real estate market, building a strong and recognizable brand on social media is crucial for attracting and retaining clients, differentiating yourself from competitors, and establishing yourself as a trusted expert in your field. By leveraging the unique features and opportunities offered by platforms such as Facebook, Instagram, LinkedIn, Pinterest, TikTok, and Twitter, you can create a cohesive and memorable brand identity that resonates with your target audience and helps drive business growth. In this chapter, we will discuss the key elements of building your real estate brand on social media and provide actionable tips for developing an authentic and engaging online presence.

Defining Your Brand Identity

Before you can effectively build your brand on social media, it is essential to have a clear understanding of your brand identity, including your unique selling proposition, core values, and target audience.

This foundational work will help guide your content creation, engagement strategies, and overall online presence. Consider the following questions when defining your brand identity:

1. What sets you apart from other real estate agents in your market?
2. What are your core values and guiding principles?
3. Who is your ideal client, and what are their needs, preferences, and pain points?
4. What tone and style best represent your personality and approach to real estate?

Consistent Visual Branding

Visual elements such as your logo, color scheme, typography, and imagery play a crucial role in building your brand on social media. By maintaining consistent visual branding across all your social media profiles and content, you can create a cohesive and memorable brand identity that helps you stand out from the crowd. Key aspects of visual branding to consider include:

- Logo: Design a professional and easily recognizable logo that represents your brand and can be used consistently across all your social media platforms and marketing materials.
- Color Scheme: Choose a color palette that aligns with your brand identity and use it consistently in your profile designs, content, and marketing materials.

- Typography: Select a consistent font style for your text content that is easy to read and visually appealing, reinforcing your brand identity.
- Imagery: Use high-quality, consistent images and videos that reflect your brand's personality, style, and values. This includes property photos, personal photos, and graphic elements.

Developing a Social Media Content Strategy

An effective content strategy is crucial for building your real estate brand on social media. By sharing valuable, engaging, and relevant content, you can establish yourself as an industry expert and foster lasting relationships with your audience. Key components of a successful content strategy include:

- Content Mix: Determine the optimal mix of content types for your brand, such as educational articles, market updates, property listings, personal stories, client testimonials, and community highlights.
- Posting Schedule: Develop a consistent posting schedule that aligns with your audience's preferences and habits, ensuring that you remain top-of-mind without overwhelming your followers.
- Content Themes: Identify content themes that resonate with your target audience and align with your brand identity, such as home staging tips, neighborhood profiles, or mortgage advice.

- Engagement: Actively engage with your audience by responding to comments, answering questions, and participating in relevant online discussions. This not only helps build rapport but also demonstrates your commitment to customer service and support.

Leveraging Platform-Specific Features

Each social media platform offers unique features and opportunities for building your real estate brand. By leveraging these platform-specific tools and functionalities, you can optimize your presence and better connect with your audience. Some examples include:

- Facebook: Utilize Facebook's groups and marketplace features to share listings, join relevant local and industry groups, and host virtual open houses or Q&A sessions using Facebook Live.
- Instagram: Take advantage of Instagram Stories and IGTV to share behind-the-scenes content, property tours, and live updates. Utilize Instagram's shopping feature to showcase listings and direct users to your website for more information.
- LinkedIn: Publish industry-related articles and engage in professional groups to position yourself as a thought leader in the real estate space. Use LinkedIn's advanced search features to identify and connect with potential clients and industry partners.

- Pinterest: Create visually appealing boards that showcase your listings, interior design inspiration, and home improvement tips. Use Pinterest's analytics tools to identify popular content and tailor your strategy accordingly.
- TikTok: Leverage TikTok's short-form video format to create engaging and entertaining content that showcases your personality, industry expertise, and unique approach to real estate.
- Twitter: Use Twitter to share timely market updates, industry news, and insights, as well as engage in real-time conversations with clients, industry professionals, and influencers.

Tracking and Measuring Success

To ensure that your social media efforts are effectively building your real estate brand, it is essential to track and measure your performance regularly. By monitoring key metrics such as engagement, reach, conversions, and click-through rates, you can identify what types of content resonate with your audience and optimize your approach accordingly. Use these insights to refine your content strategy, improve your engagement efforts, and ensure that your social media presence remains aligned with your brand identity and business goals.

Building a strong real estate brand on social media is a multifaceted endeavor that requires a clear understanding of your brand identity, consistent visual branding, a targeted content strategy, and effective platform-specific tactics.

By leveraging the unique features and opportunities offered by each social media platform, you can create a cohesive and memorable brand presence that resonates with your target audience and helps drive business growth. As you continue to refine and develop your social media presence, remember to track and measure your success to ensure that your efforts remain focused on achieving your branding and business objectives.

CHAPTER 7:

SETTING OBJECTIVES

An effective real estate social media strategy begins with setting clear and measurable objectives. These objectives serve as a roadmap for your marketing efforts, helping you allocate resources, prioritize tasks, and evaluate your success. By establishing well-defined objectives, you can focus your social media activities on achieving your desired outcomes and maximizing the return on your investment. In this chapter, we will discuss the importance of setting objectives for your real estate social media strategy, provide guidance on how to create SMART objectives, and offer examples of common goals that real estate agents may pursue on social media.

The Importance of Setting Objectives

Setting objectives is a critical step in developing a successful real estate social media strategy. By outlining specific, measurable goals, you can:

1. Focus your efforts: Objectives help you concentrate on the tasks and activities that will have the greatest impact on your desired outcomes, ensuring that you use your time and resources efficiently.
2. Measure your progress: Objectives provide a benchmark against which you can assess your performance and determine whether your social media efforts are yielding the desired results.
3. Make informed decisions: Objectives enable you to evaluate the effectiveness of your social media activities and make data-driven decisions to optimize your strategy and maximize your return on investment.
4. Communicate expectations: Clear objectives help ensure that all team members, partners, and stakeholders understand the purpose and desired outcomes of your social media efforts, facilitating collaboration and alignment.

Creating SMART Objectives

To ensure that your objectives are both actionable and achievable, it is essential to create SMART objectives. SMART is an acronym that stands for Specific, Measurable, Achievable, Relevant, and Time-bound. By adhering to the SMART criteria, you can develop objectives that are well-defined, realistic, and aligned with your overall business goals. Consider the following guidelines when creating SMART objectives:

1. Specific: Clearly define your objectives, outlining the desired outcomes, target audience, and platforms involved.
2. Measurable: Ensure that your objectives can be quantified using concrete metrics, such as engagement rates, website traffic, or lead generation.
3. Achievable: Set realistic objectives that are attainable given your resources, capabilities, and market conditions.
4. Relevant: Align your objectives with your broader business goals, ensuring that your social media efforts support your overall marketing strategy and objectives.
5. Time-bound: Establish a timeframe for achieving your objectives, allowing you to track your progress and make adjustments as needed.

Examples of Social Media Objectives for Real Estate Agents

While your specific objectives will depend on your unique business goals, market position, and target audience, some common social media objectives for real estate agents include:

- Increase brand awareness: Expand your online presence and reach a wider audience by increasing your follower count, engagement rates, and content reach.
- Generate leads: Attract potential clients and capture their contact information through targeted content, advertising campaigns, and lead magnets.
- Drive website traffic: Encourage users to visit your website for more information on your listings, services, and expertise.

- Build a community: Foster a loyal following and create a sense of community by actively engaging with your audience, sharing valuable content, and promoting user-generated content.
- Establish industry expertise: Position yourself as a thought leader and trusted resource by sharing insightful market updates, educational content, and industry news.

Setting clear and measurable objectives is an essential step in creating a successful real estate social media strategy. By establishing SMART objectives, you can focus your efforts on the activities that will yield the greatest results, track your progress, and make informed decisions to optimize your strategy. As you continue to refine your social media efforts, remember to regularly review and update your objectives to ensure they remain aligned with your evolving business goals, market conditions, and audience preferences. By maintaining a strategic and goal-oriented approach to your social media activities, you can effectively leverage these powerful platforms to build your brand, grow your business, and achieve long-term success in the competitive real estate industry.

CHAPTER 8:

DEFINING YOUR TARGET AUDIENCE

An essential component of a successful real estate social media strategy is defining your target audience. By identifying the specific group of people you aim to serve, you can tailor your content, messaging, and marketing efforts to resonate with their unique needs, preferences, and pain points. This not only increases the effectiveness of your social media activities but also enables you to build deeper connections and foster lasting relationships with potential clients. In this chapter, we will discuss the importance of defining your target audience, provide guidance on how to create detailed audience personas, and offer tips for using social media analytics to refine your understanding of your audience.

The Importance of Defining Your Target Audience

Defining your target audience is critical for several reasons:

1. Relevance: Understanding your target audience allows you to create content and messaging that is relevant and valuable to their specific needs and preferences.
2. Engagement: When your content resonates with your audience, it increases the likelihood of engagement, such as likes, comments, and shares, which can amplify your reach and visibility.
3. Conversion: Tailoring your marketing efforts to your target audience increases the chances of converting prospects into clients, as you can address their unique pain points and position your services as the ideal solution.
4. Efficiency: Focusing your efforts on a specific audience helps you use your time and resources more efficiently, as you can prioritize the platforms, content, and strategies that will have the greatest impact on your desired outcomes.

Creating Audience Personas

To effectively define your target audience, it can be helpful to create audience personas. These personas are fictional representations of your ideal clients, encompassing their demographics, psychographics, goals, challenges, and preferences. By developing detailed audience personas, you can gain a deeper understanding of your target audience and more effectively tailor your social media efforts to their needs. Consider the following factors when creating audience personas:

1. Demographics: Age, gender, location, income, occupation, education, and family status.
2. Psychographics: Interests, values, attitudes, and lifestyle preferences.
3. Goals and Challenges: What are your audience's primary objectives and pain points related to real estate? How can your services help them achieve their goals and overcome their challenges?
4. Online Behavior: Which social media platforms do they use, and how do they engage with content? What type of content do they find most valuable or appealing?
5. Communication Preferences: How do they prefer to communicate and receive information? Which channels and formats are most effective for reaching and engaging them?

Using Social Media Analytics to Refine Your Audience Understanding

Social media platforms provide a wealth of analytics and insights that can help you refine your understanding of your target audience. By regularly monitoring and analyzing these metrics, you can identify trends, preferences, and behaviors that inform your content strategy and engagement efforts. Some key metrics to track include:

- Follower Demographics: Assess the age, gender, location, and other demographic characteristics of your followers to ensure they align with your target audience.

- Content Performance: Monitor the engagement, reach, and conversion rates of your content to identify which topics, formats, and styles resonate most with your audience.
- Audience Growth: Track changes in your follower count, as well as the sources of new followers, to gauge the effectiveness of your efforts in attracting and retaining your target audience.
- Audience Feedback: Pay close attention to comments, messages, and other forms of audience feedback to gain insights into their preferences, needs, and pain points.

Defining your target audience is a critical step in developing a successful real estate social media strategy. By creating detailed audience personas and regularly monitoring social media analytics, you can ensure that your content and marketing efforts are tailored to the unique needs and preferences of your ideal clients. This not only increases the effectiveness of your social media activities but also enables you to build deeper connections and foster lasting relationships with potential clients. As you continue to refine your understanding of your target audience, remember to stay agile and adapt your social media strategy accordingly. By maintaining a strong focus on your target audience and their evolving needs, you can effectively leverage social media platforms to attract, engage, and convert prospects, driving long-term success in the competitive real estate industry.

CHAPTER 9:

CRAFTING A UNIQUE BRAND VOICE

A crucial aspect of building a strong real estate brand on social media is crafting a unique and consistent brand voice. Your brand voice is the tone, style, and personality that you convey through your content and messaging, and it plays a vital role in differentiating you from competitors and creating a memorable impression on your audience. In this chapter, we will discuss the importance of developing a distinctive brand voice, provide guidance on how to identify and define your brand voice, and offer tips for maintaining consistency across platforms and content types.

The Importance of Crafting a Unique Brand Voice

Developing a unique brand voice is essential for several reasons:

- Differentiation: A distinctive brand voice helps set you apart from competitors, allowing you to stand out in a crowded real estate market and attract your target audience.

- Memorability: A consistent and recognizable brand voice makes it easier for your audience to remember you and associate your content with your brand, increasing the likelihood that they will choose you when they need real estate services.
- Connection: A well-defined brand voice allows you to establish a deeper emotional connection with your audience by conveying your personality, values, and mission.
- Consistency: A consistent brand voice helps to create a cohesive and unified brand experience across all social media platforms, reinforcing your brand identity and increasing trust and credibility.

Identifying and Defining Your Brand Voice

To create a unique and consistent brand voice, you should first identify and define the key characteristics and traits that best represent your brand. Consider the following steps:
- Reflect on your values and mission: What are the core principles that guide your real estate business? How do you want to be perceived by your audience?
- Examine your target audience: Consider the preferences, needs, and expectations of your target audience. How can you tailor your brand voice to resonate with and appeal to them?
- Analyze your competition: Assess the brand voices of your competitors to identify gaps and opportunities in the market. What can you do differently to set yourself apart?

- Develop a list of adjectives: Create a list of adjectives that best describe your desired brand voice, such as professional, friendly, informative, or inspiring. These adjectives will serve as the foundation for your brand voice and guide your content creation.
- Create a brand voice guide: Develop a comprehensive brand voice guide that outlines the tone, style, and personality of your brand. Include examples of content that embodies your brand voice, as well as content that does not align with your desired voice.

Maintaining Consistency Across Platforms and Content Types

To ensure that your brand voice remains consistent across platforms and content types, consider the following tips:

- Train your team: Ensure that all team members involved in content creation understand and adhere to your brand voice guidelines. Regularly review and provide feedback on their work to maintain consistency.
- Adapt your voice to each platform: While your brand voice should remain consistent, it is essential to adapt your tone and style to suit the unique characteristics and user preferences of each social media platform.
- Use a consistent vocabulary: Establish a set of key phrases, terms, and messaging elements that are unique to your brand, and use them consistently across all content types and platforms.

- Review and revise content: Regularly review and revise your content to ensure it aligns with your desired brand voice. Be prepared to make adjustments as your brand evolves and your target audience's preferences change.

Crafting a unique and consistent brand voice is an essential component of building a strong real estate brand on social media. By identifying and defining your desired brand voice, and maintaining consistency across platforms and content types, you can effectively differentiate yourself from competitors, create a memorable impression on your audience, and establish deeper connections with potential clients. As you continue to develop and refine your brand voice, remember to stay true to your core values and mission, while also remaining agile and adaptive to the evolving needs and preferences of your target audience. By consistently embodying your unique brand voice in your social media content and interactions, you can leverage these powerful platforms to build a distinctive and compelling real estate brand that drives long-term success in the competitive industry.

CHAPTER 10:

DEVELOPING A CONSISTENT VISUAL IDENTITY

In addition to crafting a unique brand voice, developing a consistent visual identity is crucial for building a strong real estate brand on social media. Your visual identity encompasses the colors, fonts, imagery, and design elements that define your brand and make it easily recognizable to your audience. By establishing a cohesive visual identity, you can create a memorable and professional impression on your target audience, reinforce your brand message, and enhance the overall user experience. In this chapter, we will discuss the importance of developing a consistent visual identity, provide guidance on creating a visual identity guide, and offer tips for maintaining consistency across platforms and content types.

The Importance of Developing a Consistent Visual Identity

A consistent visual identity is essential for several reasons:
- Recognition: A cohesive and distinctive visual identity makes it easy for your audience to recognize your content and associate it with your brand,

increasing the likelihood that they will remember you and choose your services.

- Professionalism: A well-designed and consistent visual identity conveys professionalism and credibility, which can help you build trust and confidence with your audience.
- Emotional connection: A strong visual identity can evoke emotions and create a lasting impression on your audience, enhancing your brand message and fostering deeper connections.
- User experience: A consistent visual identity helps to create a cohesive and enjoyable user experience, making it more likely that your audience will engage with and share your content.

Creating a Visual Identity Guide

To develop a consistent visual identity, it's essential to create a comprehensive visual identity guide that outlines the key elements and guidelines for your brand. Consider the following components when creating your visual identity guide:

- Color palette: Choose a primary color palette that represents your brand and resonates with your target audience. Include a few complementary colors to provide variety and flexibility in your designs.
- Typography: Select a set of fonts that align with your brand personality and are legible across different platforms and devices. Consider choosing one primary font for headings and another for body text.

- Imagery: Establish guidelines for the types of images and graphics you will use in your content, such as photography styles, illustrations, and iconography. Ensure that your imagery aligns with your brand values and target audience preferences.
- Logo and branding elements: Develop a clear and versatile logo that represents your brand and can be easily adapted to various platforms and formats. Include any additional branding elements, such as patterns, textures, or shapes, that can be used to enhance your designs.
- Layout and design principles: Outline the basic layout and design principles for your content, such as whitespace, alignment, and visual hierarchy, to ensure consistency and readability.

Maintaining Consistency Across Platforms and Content Types

To ensure that your visual identity remains consistent across platforms and content types, consider the following tips:

- Train your team: Ensure that all team members involved in content creation understand and adhere to your visual identity guidelines. Provide them with access to your visual identity guide and any necessary design assets.
- Adapt your visual identity to each platform: While your visual identity should remain consistent, it is essential to adapt your design elements to suit the unique characteristics and user preferences of each social media platform.

- Use templates: Create a set of templates for different content types and platforms that incorporate your visual identity elements, making it easy for your team to produce consistent and on-brand content.
- Review and revise content: Regularly review and revise your content to ensure it aligns with your desired visual identity. Be prepared to make adjustments as your brand evolves and your target audience's preferences change.

Developing a consistent visual identity is a crucial component of building a strong real estate brand on social media. By creating a comprehensive visual identity guide and maintaining consistency across platforms and content types, you can effectively convey professionalism, evoke emotions, and create a memorable impression on your target audience. As you continue to develop and refine your visual identity, remember to stay true to your core values and mission while remaining agile and adaptive to the evolving needs and preferences of your target audience. By consistently incorporating your unique visual identity in your social media content and interactions, you can leverage these powerful platforms to build a distinctive and compelling real estate brand that drives long-term success in the competitive industry.

CHAPTER 11:

FACEBOOK FOR REAL ESTATE AGENTS

Facebook is an indispensable tool for real estate agents looking to build their brand, connect with potential clients, and generate leads. With its diverse user base and robust advertising capabilities, Facebook offers a powerful platform for showcasing properties, sharing valuable information, and fostering meaningful relationships. In this chapter, we will explore the unique features and opportunities that Facebook provides for real estate agents, as well as offer practical guidance on how to effectively use this platform to grow your business.

Setting Up a Professional Facebook Page

A professional Facebook page is the foundation of your Facebook presence and serves as the hub for all your business-related content and interactions. To set up a professional Facebook page:

- Create a separate business page: Avoid mixing personal and professional content by creating a dedicated business page separate from your personal profile.
- Choose an appropriate page name: Select a page name that accurately reflects your brand and is easy to remember. Ideally, this should include your name and "Real Estate" or your agency's name.
- Optimize your page's profile and cover photos: Use high-quality, professional images that showcase your brand and convey your brand's visual identity.
- Complete the "About" section: Fill out your page's "About" section with relevant information, such as your contact details, website, and a brief description of your services.
- Include a call-to-action (CTA) button: Add a CTA button, such as "Contact Us" or "Book a Consultation," to encourage visitors to take action.

Creating Engaging Content for Your Facebook Page

To attract and engage your audience on Facebook, focus on creating and sharing a mix of valuable, relevant, and visually appealing content. Consider the following content types:

- Property listings: Showcase your listings with high-quality photos, videos, and detailed descriptions. Use Facebook's carousel format to display multiple images and highlight different features of the property.
- Local market updates: Share regular updates on local market trends and news to position yourself as a knowledgeable and trusted resource.

- Educational content: Offer tips and insights on the home buying or selling process, home maintenance, and other real estate-related topics.
- Personal stories and behind-the-scenes content: Humanize your brand by sharing personal anecdotes, client testimonials, and behind-the-scenes glimpses of your work.
- Community engagement: Highlight local events, businesses, and attractions to demonstrate your expertise and involvement in the local community.
- Live video: Use Facebook Live to host Q&A sessions, virtual open houses, or property tours to engage with your audience in real-time.

Leveraging Facebook Ads for Real Estate Lead Generation

Facebook Ads provide a powerful tool for targeting and engaging your ideal audience, driving traffic to your website, and generating leads. To create effective Facebook Ads:

- Define your target audience: Use Facebook's targeting options to narrow down your audience based on factors such as location, age, interests, and behaviors.
- Create compelling ad creatives: Design visually appealing ads that convey your brand's visual identity and include a clear, concise message.
- Use attention-grabbing headlines: Write headlines that pique interest and encourage users to click on your ad.
- Include a strong CTA: Encourage users to take action by including a clear and compelling CTA, such as "Schedule a Viewing" or "Download Our Buyer's Guide."

- Monitor and optimize your campaigns: Regularly review your ad performance and make adjustments as needed to improve your results.

Building Relationships Through Facebook Groups

Participating in Facebook Groups allows you to connect with potential clients, network with other professionals, and establish yourself as an industry expert. To leverage Facebook Groups effectively:

- Join relevant groups: Search for local community groups, real estate groups, and other groups that align with your target audience's interests.
- Provide value: Position yourself as a helpful resource by answering questions, sharing insights, and offering expert advice. Avoid excessive self-promotion, as it can be off-putting to group members.
- Engage with other members: Interact with group members by liking, commenting on, and sharing their posts. This will help you build relationships and increase your visibility within the group.
- Share relevant content: Post useful and engaging content that demonstrates your expertise and adds value to the group, such as market updates, educational articles, and community highlights.
- Create your own group: Consider creating your own Facebook Group to establish a dedicated community around your brand. This can serve as a platform for sharing exclusive content, hosting live events, and fostering deeper connections with your audience.

Tracking Your Facebook Performance

Monitoring and analyzing your Facebook performance is crucial for understanding the effectiveness of your efforts and making data-driven decisions. Use Facebook Insights to track key metrics, such as:

- Page likes and follows: Monitor your page's growth and audience size over time.
- Reach and engagement: Measure the number of users who see and interact with your content.
- Post-performance: Analyze the performance of individual posts to identify trends and preferences among your audience.
- Click-through rates and conversions: Track the effectiveness of your ads in driving traffic to your website and generating leads.
- Audience demographics: Gain insights into the characteristics of your audience, such as age, gender, and location.

Use these metrics to refine your content strategy, optimize your ads, and improve your overall Facebook presence.

Facebook offers a powerful platform for real estate agents looking to build their brand, engage with potential clients, and generate leads. By setting up a professional Facebook page, creating valuable and engaging content, leveraging Facebook Ads, participating in Facebook Groups, and tracking your performance, you can harness the full potential of this platform to grow your real estate business. Remember to stay authentic, provide value, and adapt your strategies based on data-driven insights to achieve long-term success on Facebook.

CHAPTER 12:

SETTING UP A PROFESSIONAL PAGE

A professional Facebook business page serves as the foundation for your online presence, allowing you to showcase your expertise, engage with your target audience, and generate leads. Establishing a professional Facebook page ensures a consistent brand presence and increases your visibility. In this chapter, we will provide step-by-step guidance on how to set up a professional Facebook business page and best practices to optimize your page for success.

Creating a Professional Facebook Business Page

To set up a professional Facebook business page, follow these steps:
- Log in to your personal Facebook account.
- Click on the "Pages" tab on the left-hand side menu.
- Click on the "Create New Page" button.
- Choose an appropriate page name that accurately reflects your brand and is easy to remember.

Ideally, this should include your name and "Real Estate" or your agency's name.

- Select the "Real Estate" category for your page.
- Add a brief description of your real estate services, focusing on your unique value proposition.

Customizing Your Facebook Business Page

Once your page is created, it's time to optimize it for success:

- Profile and cover photos: Upload high-quality, professional images that showcase your brand and convey your brand's visual identity. Ensure your profile picture is easily recognizable, such as a professional headshot or your company logo. Your cover photo should provide additional context about your services or highlight a recent success story.
- Complete the "About" section: Fill out your page's "About" section with relevant information, such as your contact details, website, and a brief description of your services. This section should also include your business hours, if applicable.
- Add a call-to-action (CTA) button: Include a CTA button, such as "Contact Us" or "Book a Consultation," to encourage visitors to take action.
- Create custom tabs: Customize the tabs on your page to include relevant sections, such as "Listings," "Reviews," or "Events." This allows you to organize your content and make it easily accessible to visitors.

- Page settings: Review your page settings to ensure you have enabled features such as messaging, notifications, and visitor posts, as these will help you engage with your audience more effectively.

Best Practices for Your Facebook Business Page

- Post consistently: Develop a posting schedule to maintain a consistent presence on your page. Aim for a balance of promotional, educational, and engaging content that appeals to your target audience.
- Use visuals: Incorporate eye-catching visuals, such as images, videos, and infographics, to capture your audience's attention and enhance your content.
- Engage with your audience: Respond promptly to comments, messages, and reviews to build relationships and demonstrate your commitment to providing excellent service.
- Monitor your page insights: Regularly review your page insights to understand your audience demographics, post-performance, and overall engagement. Use this data to inform your content strategy and make improvements where necessary.
- Cross-promote your page: Increase your page's visibility by sharing it on your other social media profiles, including it in your email signature, and adding a link or Facebook icon on your website.

Setting up a professional Facebook business page is a crucial step in establishing a strong online presence for your real estate business. By creating and optimizing your page, you can effectively showcase your expertise, engage with your audience, and generate leads. Stay committed to providing valuable content, engaging with your audience, and adapting your strategies based on insights to achieve long-term success on Facebook.

CHAPTER 13:

OPTIMIZING YOUR PROFILE

Optimizing your Facebook profile plays a significant role in maximizing your online presence and attracting potential clients. A well-optimized profile not only establishes credibility but also helps to build trust with your audience. In this chapter, we will discuss various strategies and best practices to optimize your Facebook profile to drive engagement and effectively showcase your real estate expertise.

Creating an Engaging Profile and Cover Photo

Your profile and cover photos are the first visual elements your audience will see when visiting your Facebook business page. Therefore, it is essential to create engaging and professional visuals that reflect your brand's identity and convey a strong message about your services.

- Profile photo: Use a high-quality, professional headshot or your company logo that is easily recognizable.

Ensure that the image is well-lit and appropriately cropped to fit the profile photo dimensions (180x180 pixels).

- Cover photo: Choose a high-resolution image that highlights your services, showcases a recent success story, or reflects your brand's personality. You can also use a slideshow or a short video to create a more dynamic visual experience. Ensure that the cover photo dimensions are 820x312 pixels on desktop and 640x360 pixels on mobile devices.

Crafting a Compelling "About" Section

Your "About" section serves as a snapshot of your business, providing essential information about your real estate services and unique value proposition. To optimize your "About" section:

- Create a concise yet informative description that highlights your expertise, specialties, and the benefits of working with you.
- Include relevant keywords related to your services and location to improve searchability and visibility.
- Add your contact information, such as phone number, email address, and website, to make it easy for potential clients to get in touch.
- Include links to your other social media profiles to encourage cross-platform engagement.
- Update your "About" section regularly to reflect any changes in your services or areas of expertise.

Utilizing Custom Tabs and Sections

Customizing the tabs and sections on your Facebook business page allows you to organize your content and make it easily accessible to your audience. Consider adding the following sections to your page:

- Listings: Create a dedicated tab for your property listings, making it easy for potential clients to browse available properties.
- Reviews: Encourage clients to leave reviews on your page and showcase these testimonials to build trust and credibility.
- Events: Promote open houses, webinars, and other events to keep your audience informed and engaged.
- Services: Highlight the various real estate services you offer and include pricing information, if applicable.
- Custom tabs: Use custom tabs to feature specific content, such as blog posts, resources, or success stories.

Posting High-Quality, Engaging Content

A crucial aspect of optimizing your Facebook profile is consistently posting high-quality, engaging content that appeals to your target audience. Develop a content strategy that includes a mix of promotional, educational, and entertaining content:

- Property listings: Showcase your available properties with high-quality images, virtual tours, and detailed descriptions.

- Market updates: Share local market insights, trends, and news to demonstrate your expertise and keep your audience informed.
- Educational content: Offer valuable tips and advice on topics related to home buying, selling, and homeownership.
- Personal stories: Share behind-the-scenes glimpses of your daily life as a real estate agent and celebrate your successes to create a personal connection with your audience.
- Visual content: Use eye-catching visuals, such as images, videos, and infographics, to enhance your posts and boost engagement.

Engaging with Your Audience

To optimize your Facebook profile, it is essential to engage with your audience consistently. Building relationships with your followers will increase trust, loyalty, and, ultimately, the likelihood of converting them into clients. Here are some strategies for engaging with your audience:

- Respond to comments: Make an effort to reply to comments on your posts in a timely and thoughtful manner. This will demonstrate your dedication to providing excellent service and encourage further engagement.
- Address messages promptly: Respond to direct messages and inquiries as quickly as possible to show that you value your audience's time and are readily available to assist them.

- Encourage user-generated content: Invite your followers to share their experiences, photos, or stories related to your services. This will not only create a sense of community but also provide valuable social proof.
- Host Q&A sessions: Schedule regular live Q&A sessions or "Ask Me Anything" events to address your audience's questions and concerns directly.
- Monitor and respond to reviews: Keep track of the reviews on your page and respond to both positive and negative feedback. Thank your clients for their positive reviews and address any concerns or issues in a professional manner.

Analyzing and Adapting Your Strategy

Finally, optimizing your Facebook profile requires continuous analysis and adaptation of your strategy based on performance data. Use Facebook Insights to monitor your page's performance, including audience demographics, post engagement, and overall reach. Use this information to make informed decisions about your content strategy, posting frequency, and engagement tactics. Adjust your approach as needed to ensure ongoing growth and success.

Optimizing your Facebook profile is a crucial step in establishing a strong online presence for your real estate business. By creating engaging visuals, crafting a compelling "About" section, posting high-quality content, and engaging with your audience, you can effectively showcase your expertise and attract potential clients. Stay committed to analyzing your performance data and adapting your strategies to achieve long-term success on Facebook.

CHAPTER 14:

CREATING ENGAGING CONTENT

Creating engaging content for your Facebook business page is essential to capture your audience's attention, foster interaction, and generate leads. A successful content strategy combines various types of content that appeal to your target audience and showcase your real estate expertise. In this chapter, we will explore different content formats, ideas, and best practices to help you create engaging Facebook content that drives results.

Diversifying Content Formats

Using a mix of content formats keeps your audience engaged and encourages interaction. Consider incorporating the following formats into your content strategy:

- Images: Share high-quality images of your listings, local landmarks, and community events. Images should be visually appealing and reflect your brand's identity.

- Videos: Create short videos that provide insights into your services, showcase property tours, or share helpful tips. Videos are highly engaging and can boost your organic reach.
- Live streaming: Host live streaming sessions, such as Q&A sessions or virtual open houses, to interact with your audience in real-time.
- Links: Share links to relevant articles, blog posts, or resources that provide value to your audience.
- Text updates: Craft short and engaging text updates that share insights, ask questions, or celebrate your successes.

Content Ideas for Engaging Facebook Posts

To create engaging content, focus on topics that resonate with your target audience and showcase your real estate expertise. Consider the following content ideas:

- Property listings: Share your latest property listings with high-quality images, detailed descriptions, and a clear call-to-action.
- Success stories: Highlight recent sales or satisfied client testimonials to build trust and credibility.
- Market updates: Share local real estate market updates, trends, and news to demonstrate your expertise and keep your audience informed.
- Home improvement tips: Offer advice on home improvements, renovations, or DIY projects that can add value to a property.
- Neighborhood features: Showcase the highlights of the neighborhoods you serve,

such as local attractions, restaurants, schools, and parks.

- Real estate tips: Provide helpful tips for buyers, sellers, and homeowners, such as preparing a home for sale, negotiating offers, or understanding the mortgage process.
- Behind-the-scenes: Share glimpses into your daily life as a real estate agent, including office life, client meetings, and property tours.
- Personal milestones: Celebrate your achievements, such as awards, recognitions, or work anniversaries.
- Interactive content: Encourage engagement by asking open-ended questions, creating polls, or hosting giveaways.

Best Practices for Creating Engaging Facebook Content

- Prioritize quality over quantity: Focus on creating high-quality content that provides value to your audience, rather than simply posting for the sake of maintaining a consistent presence.
- Be authentic: Share content that reflects your personality and showcases your unique perspective as a real estate agent.
- Use visuals: Enhance your posts with eye-catching visuals, such as images, videos, and infographics.
- Encourage engagement: Craft your posts to encourage interaction by asking questions, requesting feedback, or inviting your audience to share their experiences.
- Leverage user-generated content: Share content created by your clients or followers, such as testimonials, photos, or stories, to create a sense of community and provide social proof.

- Optimize for mobile: Ensure that your content is easily accessible and visually appealing on mobile devices, as a significant portion of Facebook users access the platform on their smartphones.
- Monitor performance: Regularly review your Facebook Insights to understand which types of content resonate most with your audience and adjust your strategy accordingly.

Creating engaging Facebook content is crucial to building a strong online presence and driving results for your real estate business. By diversifying your content formats, focusing on topics that resonate with your target audience, and implementing best practices, you can create a successful content strategy that fosters interaction and generates leads.

Remember to stay authentic and true to your brand while continuously experimenting with different content types and ideas. Monitoring your performance and adapting your content strategy based on the insights you gather will ensure ongoing growth and success on Facebook.

By prioritizing quality, fostering engagement, and showcasing your real estate expertise through engaging content, you will not only attract potential clients but also build lasting relationships that can lead to future business opportunities. Stay committed to creating valuable and engaging content that positions you as a trusted expert in your niche, and your Facebook business page will become an essential tool for growing your real estate business.

CHAPTER 15:

LEVERAGING FACEBOOK ADS

Facebook Ads offer a powerful and cost-effective way for real estate agents to reach their target audience, generate leads, and grow their business. With its extensive targeting capabilities and flexible ad formats, Facebook Ads can help you create highly targeted campaigns that drive results. In this chapter, we will explore the benefits of Facebook Ads, discuss various ad formats, and provide strategies for creating effective campaigns that meet your real estate objectives.

Benefits of Facebook Ads for Real Estate Agents

Facebook Ads provide several advantages to real estate agents, including:

- Precise targeting: Facebook Ads allow you to target your audience based on demographics, interests, behaviors, and location, ensuring that your ads reach the right people.
- Wide reach: With over 2.8 billion monthly active users, Facebook offers a vast audience that you can tap into to expand your reach.

- Cost-effective advertising: Facebook Ads operate on a bidding system, allowing you to control your ad spend and achieve a high return on investment (ROI).
- Measurable results: Facebook Ads Manager provides detailed analytics and reporting, enabling you to track the performance of your campaigns and optimize them for better results.
- Flexible ad formats: Facebook offers a variety of ad formats, such as image, video, carousel, and slideshow ads, that cater to different objectives and user preferences.

Facebook Ad Formats for Real Estate Agents

Facebook offers several ad formats that real estate agents can leverage to achieve their marketing goals:

- Image ads: Use high-quality images to showcase your listings, promote open houses, or share market updates.
- Video ads: Create engaging video content that offers virtual tours, shares tips, or highlights your expertise.
- Carousel ads: Feature multiple images or videos within a single ad, allowing you to showcase multiple properties or highlight various aspects of a single listing.
- Slideshow ads: Combine images, text, and music to create a dynamic, lightweight ad that tells a compelling story about your services or listings.
- Lead generation ads: Collect lead information directly within the Facebook platform using pre-filled forms, making it easy for potential clients to express interest in your services.

- Messenger ads: Engage with your audience through Facebook Messenger, offering personalized property recommendations or answering questions in real-time.

Creating Effective Facebook Ad Campaigns

To create effective Facebook ad campaigns, follow these steps:
- Define your objectives: Identify the goals of your campaign, such as generating leads, driving traffic to your website, or promoting an open house.
- Choose the right ad format: Select the ad format that aligns with your objectives and best showcases your content.
- Target your audience: Use Facebook's targeting options to reach your ideal audience, considering factors such as location, demographics, interests, and behaviors.
- Set your budget and schedule: Determine your daily or lifetime budget and select a schedule for your campaign, such as running continuously or during specific dates.
- Design engaging creatives: Develop eye-catching visuals and compelling ad copy that resonate with your target audience and convey your value proposition.
- Optimize your landing pages: Ensure that your website or landing pages are optimized for conversions, providing a seamless user experience and clear calls-to-action.
- Monitor and analyze performance: Use Facebook Ads Manager to track the performance of your campaigns, adjusting your targeting, creatives, or budget as needed to improve results.

Tips for Optimizing Facebook Ads

To maximize the effectiveness of your Facebook Ads, consider these optimization tips:

- Test multiple ad variations: Experiment with different headlines, images, and ad formats to determine which combinations resonate most with your audience.
- Use engaging visuals: Incorporate high-quality images or videos that capture attention and showcase your listings or services in the best possible light.
- Include clear calls-to-action: Guide your audience toward the desired action, such as visiting your website, signing up for a newsletter, or contacting you for a consultation.
- Focus on mobile optimization: Ensure that your ads and landing pages are optimized for mobile devices, as a significant portion of Facebook users access the platform on their smartphones.
- Utilize retargeting strategies: Create custom audiences based on user interactions with your website or previous ads, allowing you to retarget potential clients who have already shown interest in your services.
- Monitor and adjust targeting: Regularly review your targeting settings and adjust them as needed to improve the performance of your campaigns.
- Leverage Facebook Pixel: Install the Facebook Pixel on your website to track conversions, optimize your ads, and build custom audiences based on website visitors.

Leveraging Facebook Ads can significantly enhance your real estate marketing efforts by providing a cost-effective, targeted, and measurable way to reach your audience and achieve your objectives. By choosing the right ad formats, creating engaging creatives, and optimizing your campaigns based on performance data, you can drive results and grow your real estate business.

Stay committed to testing and refining your Facebook Ads strategy to ensure ongoing success and maximize your return on investment. As you gain experience and insights from your campaigns, you'll be better equipped to create compelling, targeted ads that resonate with your audience and generate valuable leads for your real estate business.

CHAPTER 16:

UTILIZING FACEBOOK GROUPS AND EVENTS

Facebook Groups and Events offer real estate agents unique opportunities to build a community, foster engagement, and showcase their expertise. By leveraging these features, you can create meaningful connections with your target audience, provide valuable content, and generate leads. In this chapter, we will discuss the benefits of using Facebook Groups and Events and provide strategies for effectively implementing them in your real estate marketing efforts.

Benefits of Facebook Groups for Real Estate Agents

Facebook Groups provide several advantages for real estate agents:

- Community building: Groups allow you to create a dedicated space where you can connect with your audience, share valuable content, and foster a sense of community.

- Increased engagement: Group members are more likely to see and engage with your content, as group posts typically receive higher visibility than business page posts.
- Targeted discussions: You can create topic-specific groups that cater to specific interests or needs, such as local neighborhood groups or groups for first-time homebuyers.
- Reputation building: By actively participating in groups, you can position yourself as a knowledgeable and helpful resource within your niche, building trust and credibility.

Strategies for Using Facebook Groups

To effectively leverage Facebook Groups in your real estate marketing efforts, consider the following strategies:

- Create your own group: Establish a group that aligns with your target audience's interests, such as a neighborhood community group or a group for local homebuyers and sellers.
- Join existing groups: Participate in relevant local and real estate-related groups, engaging in discussions, sharing valuable content, and offering your expertise.
- Provide valuable content: Share informative articles, market updates, and helpful tips that resonate with your group members and showcase your real estate knowledge.
- Encourage engagement: Foster a sense of community by asking questions, creating polls, and encouraging members to share their experiences and insights.
- Promote your services: Occasionally promote your services, open houses, or listings within the group, ensuring that your promotional content is balanced with valuable, non-promotional content.

- Monitor and moderate: Regularly monitor your group to ensure that discussions remain relevant and respectful, and moderate content as needed.

Benefits of Facebook Events for Real Estate Agents

Facebook Events offer several advantages for real estate agents:

- Increased visibility: Events receive higher visibility in users' News Feeds, increasing the likelihood of your audience seeing and engaging with your event content.
- Easy sharing: Facebook Events can be easily shared by attendees, helping to expand your reach and generate interest in your event.
- RSVP tracking: Facebook Events allow you to track RSVPs, providing insights into your event's attendance and helping you plan accordingly.

Strategies for Using Facebook Events

To effectively leverage Facebook Events in your real estate marketing efforts, consider the following strategies:

- Create engaging events: Host events that appeal to your target audience, such as open houses, homebuyer seminars, or community gatherings.
- Optimize event details: Ensure that your event description, cover photo, and other details are engaging and informative, providing a clear overview of the event and its value.

- Promote your event: Share your event on your business page, in relevant groups, and through other marketing channels to generate interest and boost attendance.
- Encourage sharing: Ask your attendees to share the event with their networks, increasing its visibility and reach.
- Follow up with attendees: After the event, connect with attendees to thank them for attending, gather feedback, and nurture potential leads.

Utilizing Facebook Groups and Events can significantly enhance your real estate marketing efforts by fostering community, increasing engagement, and showcasing your expertise. By implementing the strategies discussed in this chapter, you can effectively leverage these features to create meaningful connections with your target audience and generate valuable leads for your real estate business.

Stay committed to providing valuable content, engaging with your audience, and continuously refining your approach to Facebook Groups and Events. As you build a strong community and demonstrate your expertise, you will not only attract potential clients but also strengthen your reputation as a trusted and knowledgeable real estate agent.

By investing time and effort into Facebook Groups and Events, you can create a powerful and sustainable marketing channel that supports your real estate business's growth and success. Embrace the opportunities these features offer and harness their potential to enhance your online presence, foster lasting relationships, and drive results for your real estate business.

CHAPTER 17:

YOUTUBE FOR REAL ESTATE AGENTS

YouTube, as the world's second-largest search engine, offers real estate agents a powerful platform to showcase their expertise, properties, and services through video content. With over 2 billion monthly active users, YouTube provides a vast audience and significant opportunities for real estate agents to reach potential clients, generate leads, and grow their businesses. In this chapter, we will explore the benefits of using YouTube, discuss effective video content ideas, and provide strategies for creating and optimizing your YouTube channel.

Benefits of YouTube for Real Estate Agents

YouTube offers several advantages for real estate agents:
- Enhanced visibility: YouTube videos often appear in Google search results, providing an additional opportunity for your content to be discovered by potential clients.

- Engaging content format: Video content is highly engaging, allowing you to showcase your properties, services, and expertise in a compelling and immersive way.
- Establishing authority: By creating valuable and informative video content, you can position yourself as an expert in your field and build trust with your audience.
- Wide reach: YouTube's vast user base offers a significant opportunity to expand your reach and connect with potential clients.

Video Content Ideas for Real Estate Agents

To effectively leverage YouTube, consider creating various types of video content, such as:

- Property tours: Showcase your listings through virtual tours that highlight the property's unique features and amenities.
- Market updates: Share local market updates, trends, and insights to keep your audience informed and showcase your expertise.
- How-to videos: Create educational content, such as home buying and selling tips, home improvement ideas, and mortgage advice.
- Neighborhood guides: Offer virtual tours of local neighborhoods, discussing amenities, schools, and other attractions.
- Client testimonials: Share stories and experiences from satisfied clients to build credibility and trust.
- Agent introductions: Introduce yourself and your team, discussing your background, services, and unique value proposition.

Creating and Optimizing Your YouTube Channel

To create and optimize your YouTube channel, follow these steps:

- Set up your channel: Create a YouTube channel using your Google account, ensuring that it is linked to your real estate business.
- Customize your channel: Add branded channel art, a profile picture, and a compelling channel description that highlights your expertise and services.
- Organize your content: Create playlists to categorize your videos by topic, making it easier for viewers to navigate your channel and find relevant content.
- Optimize your video titles and descriptions: Use keyword-rich titles and descriptions to improve the searchability of your videos and increase their visibility in search results.
- Add tags: Include relevant tags to help YouTube understand your video's content and improve its discoverability.
- Use custom thumbnails: Create eye-catching custom thumbnails that accurately represent your video content and entice viewers to click and watch.
- Include calls-to-action: Encourage viewers to take action, such as subscribing to your channel, visiting your website, or contacting you for more information.

Tips for Creating Engaging YouTube Videos

To create engaging and effective YouTube videos, consider these tips:

- Invest in quality equipment: Use a good-quality camera, microphone, and lighting to ensure that your videos look and sound professional.
- Plan your content: Outline your video's structure and main points to ensure a coherent and well-organized presentation.
- Keep it concise: Aim to keep your videos relatively short and to the point, focusing on delivering valuable and engaging content.
- Engage your audience: Speak directly to your viewers, using a conversational tone and maintaining eye contact with the camera.
- Edit your videos: Use video editing software to enhance your videos by adding transitions, text overlays, and background music, as well as trimming any unnecessary footage.
- Be consistent: Publish videos regularly and maintain a consistent style and tone across your content, reinforcing your brand identity.
- Collaborate with others: Consider collaborating with other real estate professionals, local businesses, or influencers to expand your reach and offer diverse perspectives.
- Encourage engagement: Invite viewers to comment, like, and share your videos, fostering interaction and building a sense of community.

Promoting Your YouTube Videos

To maximize the visibility and reach of your YouTube videos, consider the following promotion strategies:

- Share on social media: Promote your videos on your other social media platforms, such as Facebook, Instagram, and LinkedIn, to drive traffic to your YouTube channel.
- Embed videos on your website: Feature your YouTube videos on your website, such as in blog posts or on your property listings pages, to provide engaging content for your website visitors.
- Include in email marketing: Share your YouTube videos in your email newsletters or promotional emails, offering valuable content to your subscribers.
- Utilize YouTube advertising: Consider running YouTube ads, such as TrueView or Discovery ads, to reach a wider audience and drive views to your videos.
- Collaborate and cross-promote: Partner with other real estate professionals or local businesses to cross-promote each other's YouTube content, expanding your reach and offering mutual support.

YouTube offers real estate agents a powerful and engaging platform to showcase their expertise, properties, and services through video content. By creating valuable and informative videos, optimizing your YouTube channel, and promoting your content effectively, you can reach a vast audience, generate leads, and grow your real estate business.

Embrace the opportunities that YouTube provides, and invest time and effort in developing a successful video marketing strategy. As you gain experience and refine your approach, you will be better positioned to create compelling, engaging content that resonates with your audience and drives results for your real estate business.

CHAPTER 18:

CHANNEL CREATION

Creating a successful YouTube channel requires careful planning and attention to detail. A well-structured, professional, and engaging channel will help you attract and retain viewers, build credibility, and grow your real estate business. In this chapter, we will guide you through the steps of setting up your YouTube channel, customizing it to reflect your brand, and optimizing it for maximum visibility and engagement.

Setting Up Your YouTube Channel

Follow these steps to set up your YouTube channel:
- Create a Google account: If you do not already have one, create a Google account to access YouTube and other Google services.
- Sign in to YouTube: Log in to YouTube using your Google account credentials.
- Create a new channel: Navigate to your YouTube account settings, click on "Create a channel," and select "Get started."

Choose the "Business or other name" option and enter your real estate business name.

- Review and agree to YouTube's terms and conditions: Read and agree to YouTube's terms of service and community guidelines to proceed with creating your channel.

Customizing Your YouTube Channel

To create a professional and consistent visual identity for your YouTube channel, follow these customization steps:

- Add a profile picture: Upload a high-quality profile picture that represents your real estate brand, such as your logo or a professional headshot.
- Design channel art: Create a visually appealing channel banner that reflects your brand identity and includes essential information, such as your tagline, contact details, and social media handles.
- Write a compelling channel description: Craft a channel description that highlights your expertise, services, and unique value proposition. Include relevant keywords to improve searchability and consider adding links to your website and social media profiles.
- Add links to your website and social media profiles: Include links to your website, Facebook, Instagram, and other relevant platforms in the "About" section of your channel to make it easy for viewers to connect with you.

Organizing Your YouTube Channel

An organized and easy-to-navigate channel will help viewers find and engage with your content.

To optimize your channel structure, consider the following:

- Create playlists: Organize your videos into thematic playlists, making it easy for viewers to find relevant content.
- Customize your channel layout: Arrange your channel homepage to showcase your best content, highlight specific playlists, or feature recently uploaded videos.
- Use sections: Utilize YouTube sections to group similar content together and make it easier for viewers to explore your channel.

Channel Optimization

To maximize the visibility and searchability of your YouTube channel, follow these optimization steps:

1. Include relevant keywords: Research relevant keywords related to your real estate business and incorporate them into your channel description, video titles, and video descriptions.
2. Utilize tags: Add relevant tags to your videos to help YouTube understand your content and improve its discoverability.
3. Create custom thumbnails: Design eye-catching custom thumbnails for each video, accurately representing the content and enticing viewers to watch.
4. Add captions and subtitles: Include accurate captions and subtitles to make your videos accessible to a broader audience and improve their searchability.

Creating a successful YouTube channel requires planning, customization, and optimization to attract and retain viewers. By following the steps outlined in this chapter, you can establish a professional and engaging YouTube channel that showcases your real estate expertise, properties, and services.

With a well-structured and visually appealing channel, you can effectively leverage the power of YouTube to connect with potential clients, generate leads, and grow your real estate business. Stay committed to producing high-quality, engaging content and continuously refining your channel to maximize its impact and reach.

CHAPTER 19:

VIDEO PRODUCTION BEST PRACTICES

Producing high-quality, engaging, and informative videos is essential to building a successful YouTube channel for your real estate business. In this chapter, we will explore best practices for video production, covering topics such as planning, equipment, filming techniques, and editing, to help you create professional and impactful video content.

Planning Your Video Content

Effective planning is crucial for creating engaging and well-organized videos. Consider the following steps when planning your video content:

- Define your objectives: Determine the purpose and goals of your video, such as showcasing a property, providing market updates, or sharing tips and advice.
- Research your target audience: Understand your audience's preferences, needs, and pain points to create content that resonates with them.

- Develop a script or outline: Create a script or outline to ensure a coherent and well-structured presentation of your content.
- Choose a location: Select a suitable filming location that enhances your video content and aligns with your brand image.

Video Production Equipment

Investing in quality equipment is essential for producing professional-looking videos. Consider the following equipment:

1. Camera: Use a high-quality camera capable of recording in at least 1080p resolution, ensuring sharp and clear visuals.
2. Microphone: Choose a good-quality external microphone to capture clear and crisp audio, minimizing background noise and echo.
3. Lighting: Utilize natural light or invest in professional lighting equipment to create well-lit videos with balanced exposure.
4. Tripod or stabilizer: Use a tripod or stabilizer to keep your camera steady, avoiding shaky footage.

Filming Techniques

Employing effective filming techniques will help you create visually appealing and engaging videos. Consider the following tips:

- Composition: Use the rule of thirds to create balanced and visually appealing compositions.
- Framing: Frame your shots to focus on the subject and eliminate distracting elements.

- Movement: Incorporate camera movement, such as pans, tilts, or slides, to create dynamic and engaging visuals.
- B-roll: Capture supplementary footage, such as close-ups, aerial shots, or cutaways, to enhance your storytelling and provide visual variety.

Editing Your Videos

Editing is a crucial step in the video production process, allowing you to refine your footage and create a polished final product. Consider the following editing tips:

- Choose suitable editing software: Select a video editing software that meets your needs and skill level, such as Adobe Premiere Pro, Final Cut Pro, or iMovie.
- Trim and arrange footage: Edit your footage to remove any unnecessary or repetitive content, and arrange clips in a logical sequence.
- Add transitions: Use transitions to smoothly connect different shots and create a cohesive viewing experience.
- Enhance audio: Adjust audio levels, remove background noise, and add background music to create a balanced and professional audio mix.
- Incorporate text and graphics: Add text overlays, lower thirds, or graphics to emphasize key points, provide context, or enhance your storytelling.
- Color correction and grading: Adjust color balance, saturation, and contrast to create a consistent and visually appealing look across your footage.

- Add captions and subtitles: Include accurate captions and subtitles to make your videos accessible to a broader audience and improve searchability.

Following video production best practices will help you create high-quality, engaging, and professional content for your YouTube channel. By investing in quality equipment, employing effective filming techniques, and refining your footage through editing, you can create compelling videos that showcase your real estate expertise, properties, and services.

As you continue to create and share videos on your YouTube channel, consistently evaluate and refine your production process. Embrace feedback from your audience and stay up-to-date with industry trends and best practices. By doing so, you will be better positioned to produce content that resonates with viewers, generates leads, and drives results for your real estate business.

In the end, your commitment to producing engaging and informative content will not only strengthen your online presence but also contribute to your reputation as a knowledgeable and trustworthy real estate professional.

CHAPTER 20:

OPTIMIZATION TECHNIQUES

To maximize the reach and impact of your YouTube videos, it is essential to optimize them for searchability, engagement, and audience retention. In this chapter, we will explore YouTube video optimization techniques, covering topics such as keyword research, metadata, thumbnails, and audience engagement strategies.

Keyword Research

Identifying and utilizing relevant keywords is crucial for improving the searchability of your videos. Consider the following steps for keyword research:

- Identify your target audience: Understand your audience's preferences, needs, and pain points to determine the keywords they are likely to search for.

- Use keyword research tools: Utilize keyword research tools, such as Google Keyword Planner, TubeBuddy, or vidIQ, to identify relevant and high-performing keywords in the real estate niche.
- Analyze competitors: Examine the keywords used by successful real estate channels and videos to gain insights and inspiration.
- Create a keyword list: Compile a list of relevant keywords to incorporate into your video metadata, ensuring consistency and searchability.

Metadata Optimization

Optimizing your video metadata, including titles, descriptions, and tags, will improve searchability and engagement. Consider the following tips:

1. Craft compelling titles: Write attention-grabbing and informative titles that include your target keywords, accurately represent your video content, and encourage viewers to click.
2. Write detailed descriptions: Create comprehensive and keyword-rich descriptions that provide context and summarize the content of your video. Include links to your website, social media profiles, and relevant resources.
3. Utilize tags: Add relevant tags to your videos, incorporating your target keywords and related terms to help YouTube understand your content and improve its discoverability.
4. Include timestamps: Add timestamps to your video description, allowing viewers to navigate your content easily and find specific sections of interest.

Custom Thumbnails

Designing eye-catching and informative custom thumbnails will help attract viewers and improve click-through rates. Consider the following thumbnail design tips:

1. Use high-quality images: Choose sharp and clear images that accurately represent your video content and capture the viewer's attention.
2. Incorporate text overlays: Add concise and descriptive text overlays to provide additional context and emphasize key points.
3. Maintain a consistent style: Design thumbnails with a consistent visual style, including font, colors, and layout, to reinforce your brand identity.
4. Test different designs: Experiment with various thumbnail designs and monitor performance to determine which styles resonate most with your audience.
5. You can utilize www.Canva.com to create visually creative thumbnails.

Audience Engagement Strategies

Fostering audience engagement is crucial for boosting video performance and building a loyal following. Consider the following engagement strategies:

- Encourage interaction: Invite viewers to comment, like, and share your videos, fostering a sense of community and promoting discussion.

- Encourage interaction: Invite viewers to comment, like, and share your videos, fostering a sense of community and promoting discussion.
- Respond to comments: Engage with your audience by responding to comments, answering questions, and acknowledging feedback.
- Use end screens and annotations: Utilize end screens and annotations to promote related videos, playlists, or your channel, encouraging viewers to continue watching.
- Incorporate calls-to-action: Include clear and compelling calls-to-action in your videos, prompting viewers to subscribe, visit your website, or follow you on social media.

Monitoring Video Performance

Regularly analyzing your video performance will help you identify areas for improvement and refine your optimization strategies. Monitor the following YouTube Analytics metrics:

- Views and watch time: Track the number of views and watch time to gauge the overall popularity and engagement of your videos.
- Audience retention: Monitor audience retention rates to identify which parts of your videos are most engaging and where viewers are dropping off.
- Traffic sources: Analyze traffic sources to determine how viewers are discovering your videos and which platforms are driving the most traffic.
- Demographics and viewer behavior: Examine demographic data and viewer behavior patterns to gain insights into your target audience and their preferences.

- Click-through rate (CTR): Monitor the CTR of your video thumbnails to assess their effectiveness in attracting viewers.
- Engagement metrics: Analyze likes, dislikes, comments, and shares to evaluate how well your content resonates with your audience and drives interaction.

Continuous Improvement and Adaptation

As you continue to create and optimize your YouTube videos, embrace a mindset of continuous improvement and adaptation. Evaluate your video performance regularly, experiment with new optimization techniques, and stay up-to-date with industry trends and best practices.

By consistently refining your optimization strategies and adapting to the ever-changing YouTube landscape, you will be better positioned to maximize the reach and impact of your real estate videos, ultimately driving leads and growing your business.

Optimizing your YouTube videos is a crucial component of building a successful real estate channel. By employing effective keyword research, metadata optimization, thumbnail design, audience engagement strategies, and performance monitoring, you can create content that attracts and retains viewers, boosts your online presence, and supports your business goals. As you continue to optimize your videos, stay committed to learning, adapting, and refining your approach, ensuring long-term success in the dynamic world of YouTube.

CHAPTER 21:

PROMOTIONAL STRATEGIES

Creating high-quality and optimized videos is only half the battle when it comes to building a successful YouTube channel for your real estate business. To maximize the impact of your content, it is essential to implement effective promotional strategies that drive views, subscriptions, and engagement. In this chapter, we will explore various YouTube promotional strategies, including cross-platform promotion, collaboration, and advertising.

Cross-Platform Promotion

Leveraging your existing online presence is a cost-effective way to drive traffic to your YouTube channel. Consider the following cross-platform promotion techniques:

- Promote on your website: Embed your YouTube videos on your website, such as in blog posts, property listings, or a dedicated video gallery, to increase visibility and encourage visitors to watch your content.

- Share on social media: Regularly share your YouTube videos on your social media profiles, such as Facebook, Instagram, Twitter, and LinkedIn, to reach a broader audience and drive traffic to your channel.
- Include in email marketing: Feature your videos in email newsletters, property updates, or other marketing communications, providing valuable content for your subscribers and promoting your channel.
- Utilize online forums and communities: Share your videos in relevant online forums, groups, or communities, such as real estate discussion boards or local Facebook groups, to reach a targeted audience and drive engagement.

Collaborating with Others

Collaborating with other real estate professionals, influencers, or local businesses can help you reach new audiences and expand your online presence. Consider the following collaboration ideas:

- Partner with other real estate agents: Collaborate with other agents to create co-branded content, such as property tours, market updates, or interviews, showcasing your combined expertise and expanding your reach.
- Work with local influencers: Partner with local influencers or bloggers to create content that highlights your services, properties, or community involvement, leveraging their audience to drive traffic to your channel.

- Feature local businesses: Create videos that showcase local businesses, attractions, or events, providing valuable content for your audience and fostering relationships with local partners.
- Participate in industry events and conferences: Attend industry events, conferences, or webinars, and create content around your experiences, positioning yourself as an industry thought leader and connecting with other professionals.

YouTube Advertising

Investing in YouTube advertising can help you reach a larger audience and drive targeted traffic to your channel. Consider the following YouTube advertising options:

- YouTube TrueView ads: Run TrueView in-stream or discovery ads to promote your videos or channel, targeting your desired audience based on demographics, interests, or behaviors.
- Google Ads: Use Google Ads to create video campaigns that target specific keywords, placements, or audience segments, driving targeted traffic to your YouTube content.
- Remarketing: Set up remarketing campaigns to target viewers who have previously interacted with your videos or channel, encouraging them to return and engage further.

Encouraging Audience Participation

Fostering a sense of community and encouraging audience participation can help drive engagement, loyalty, and word-of-mouth promotion.

Consider the following audience participation strategies:

1. Host contests and giveaways: Organize contests or giveaways that require viewers to subscribe, comment, or share your videos, driving engagement and channel growth.
2. Create user-generated content: Invite your audience to submit their own videos, photos, or stories, featuring their contributions in your content and fostering a sense of community.
3. Ask for feedback: Encourage viewers to share their thoughts, suggestions, or questions in the comments section, and actively engage with their input, demonstrating your commitment to your audience.

Effective YouTube promotional strategies are crucial for maximizing the reach and impact of your real estate videos. By leveraging cross-platform promotion, collaboration, advertising, and audience participation, you can drive targeted traffic, increase engagement, and grow your online presence. As you implement these promotional strategies, be prepared to adapt and refine your approach based on performance, audience feedback, and industry trends, ensuring your YouTube channel's long-term success and supporting your real estate business goals.

CHAPTER 22:

PINTEREST FOR REAL ESTATE AGENTS

Pinterest is a powerful visual platform that can be an invaluable tool for real estate agents looking to showcase their properties, share valuable content, and generate leads. In this chapter, we will explore the potential of Pinterest for real estate agents and provide guidance on creating an effective Pinterest presence, designing eye-catching pins, and employing strategies to drive traffic and engagement.

Setting Up Your Pinterest Business Account

To get started on Pinterest, create a business account that provides access to analytics, advertising options, and other valuable features. Consider the following steps when setting up your business account:

- Sign up for a business account: Visit the Pinterest for Business page and sign up using your business email or convert an existing personal account to a business account.

- Complete your profile: Add a professional profile picture, a concise and keyword-rich description of your real estate services, and a link to your website.
- Claim your website: Claim your website on Pinterest to gain access to analytics, enable rich pins, and display your website's favicon on your pins.
- Configure settings: Review your account settings and configure your privacy, notifications, and other preferences.

Creating and Organizing Boards

Boards are the foundation of your Pinterest presence, allowing you to organize and categorize your content. Consider the following tips for creating and organizing boards:

1. Develop a content strategy: Determine the types of content you will share on Pinterest, such as property listings, home staging tips, neighborhood guides, or real estate infographics.
2. Create relevant boards: Develop boards that reflect your content strategy and cater to the interests of your target audience. Ensure each board has a descriptive title and an informative description containing relevant keywords.
3. Organize and curate content: Add pins to your boards, either by uploading original content or by repinning from other users. Maintain a balance between your own content and curated content from other sources.
4. Keep boards up-to-date: Regularly update your boards, adding new content and archiving outdated pins to keep your Pinterest presence fresh and engaging.

Designing Eye-Catching Pins

The success of your Pinterest strategy largely depends on the quality and appeal of your pins. Consider the following design tips for creating eye-catching pins:

1. Use high-quality images: Choose clear, well-lit, and visually appealing images that showcase your properties or convey your content effectively.
2. Opt for vertical images: Design pins with a vertical aspect ratio (such as 2:3 or 1:2.1), as these formats perform better on Pinterest's grid layout.
3. Add text overlays: Incorporate concise and informative text overlays on your pins to provide context and emphasize key points.
4. Maintain a consistent style: Develop a consistent visual style for your pins, including colors, fonts, and layout, to reinforce your brand identity and create a cohesive look across your content.

Optimizing Pins for Search

Pinterest functions as a visual search engine, making it essential to optimize your pins for searchability. Consider the following search optimization tips:

- Write keyword-rich descriptions: Craft informative and keyword-rich descriptions for your pins to improve their discoverability in search results.

- Utilize hashtags: Include relevant hashtags in your pin descriptions to help users find your content more easily.
- Optimize your website for rich pins: Enable rich pins on your website, which display additional information from your site on your pins, such as property prices or article titles.
- Monitor Pinterest Analytics: Regularly review your Pinterest Analytics to gain insights into your content performance, audience preferences, and search trends.

Promotional Strategies

To maximize the reach and impact of your Pinterest presence, employ effective promotional strategies that drive traffic, engagement, and lead generation. Consider the following promotional techniques:

- Cross-promote on other platforms: Share your Pinterest content on your website, social media profiles, and email marketing campaigns to increase visibility and drive traffic to your Pinterest account.
- Engage with other users: Follow, like, comment, and repin content from other Pinterest users, particularly those within your niche or local community, to build relationships and increase your visibility.
- Collaborate with influencers: Partner with local influencers, bloggers, or other real estate professionals to create collaborative boards or share content, expanding your reach and fostering mutually beneficial relationships.

- Utilize Pinterest advertising: Leverage Pinterest's advertising options, such as Promoted Pins, to reach a larger audience and drive targeted traffic to your content.
- Participate in group boards: Join relevant group boards within the real estate niche or your local community to share your content with a broader audience and increase engagement.

Measuring Success and Refining Your Strategy

Continuously monitor your Pinterest performance and adapt your strategy based on data-driven insights. Consider the following metrics to assess your success and identify areas for improvement:

1. Impressions and reach: Monitor the number of impressions and reach of your pins to gauge your content's visibility and potential audience.
2. Saves and repins: Track the number of saves and repins your content receives to assess its popularity and shareability.
3. Clicks and traffic: Measure the number of clicks your pins receive and the resulting traffic to your website to evaluate the effectiveness of your Pinterest strategy in driving leads and conversions.
4. Follower growth: Monitor your follower growth over time to assess the success of your promotional efforts and the appeal of your content.

Pinterest offers real estate agents a unique opportunity to showcase their properties, share valuable content, and connect with potential clients through a highly visual platform. By creating a compelling and well-organized Pinterest presence, designing eye-catching and optimized pins, and implementing effective promotional strategies, you can harness the power of Pinterest to drive traffic, engagement, and leads for your real estate business. As you continue to refine your Pinterest strategy, stay committed to learning, adapting, and evolving based on performance data and industry trends, ensuring the ongoing success of your Pinterest marketing efforts.

CHAPTER 23:

CREATING CAPTIVATING PINS

A crucial aspect of a successful Pinterest marketing strategy for real estate agents lies in the ability to create captivating pins that grab the attention of users, drive engagement, and generate leads. In this chapter, we will delve into the various elements of designing captivating Pinterest pins, including image selection, text overlays, branding, and pin optimization.

Image Selection

Choosing the right images for your pins is the foundation of creating captivating content. Consider the following tips when selecting images:

- Use high-quality images: Opt for high-resolution, well-lit, and visually appealing images that showcase your properties, services, or expertise in the best possible light.
- Showcase property highlights. Feature images that highlight the unique selling points of your properties, such as stunning views, spacious rooms, or luxurious amenities.

- Utilize lifestyle imagery: Incorporate images that showcase the lifestyle and experience associated with your properties or services, creating an emotional connection with your audience.
- Mix up your visuals: Diversify your content by including different types of visuals, such as infographics, before-and-after transformations, or animated GIFs, to keep your audience engaged.

Text Overlays

Adding text overlays to your pins can provide context, highlight key information, and create a stronger visual impact. Consider the following tips for crafting effective text overlays:

1. Keep it concise: Use short and punchy headlines or phrases that convey your message quickly and efficiently.
2. Use legible fonts: Choose clear and readable fonts that complement your visuals and maintain consistency with your brand identity.
3. Utilize contrasting colors: Ensure your text is easily visible by using contrasting colors that stand out against the background.
4. Incorporate a call-to-action: Encourage users to take action by including a clear and compelling call-to-action, such as "Click for more info" or "Schedule a tour."

Branding and Consistency

Maintaining a consistent visual identity across your pins can strengthen your brand recognition and create a cohesive user experience.

Consider the following tips for incorporating branding elements:

1. Use consistent colors: Employ a color palette that aligns with your brand identity and reinforces your brand message.
2. Incorporate your logo: Add your logo or watermark to your pins to increase brand recognition and protect your original content.
3. Maintain a consistent style: Adopt a consistent style for your pins, including layout, typography, and imagery, to create a cohesive look and feel across your content.
4. Develop branded templates: Create templates for your pins that incorporate your brand elements, ensuring consistency and saving time in the design process.

Pin Optimization

Optimizing your pins for search and engagement is essential for maximizing their potential reach and impact. Consider the following tips for pin optimization:

- Use vertical images: Design pins with a vertical aspect ratio (such as 2:3 or 1:2.1) to ensure they display optimally on Pinterest's grid layout.
- Write keyword-rich descriptions: Craft informative and keyword-rich descriptions for your pins to improve their discoverability in search results and provide context for users.
- Utilize hashtags: Include relevant hashtags in your pin descriptions to help users find your content more easily.

- Enable rich pins: Enable rich pins on your website to display additional information from your site on your pins, such as property prices or article titles.

Creating captivating Pinterest pins is a vital component of a successful Pinterest marketing strategy for real estate agents. By focusing on image selection, text overlays, branding, and pin optimization, you can craft pins that grab the attention of users, drive engagement, and generate leads for your real estate business. As you continue to develop and refine your Pinterest pin design skills, remain open to experimentation and adaptation based on performance data and audience feedback. By staying committed to creating visually appealing, informative, and engaging pins, you can harness the full potential of Pinterest as a powerful marketing tool for your real estate business.

CHAPTER 24:

ORGANIZING BOARDS

An organized and well-curated Pinterest presence is key to attracting and retaining your target audience, as well as positioning yourself as an authority in the real estate industry. In this chapter, we will explore effective strategies for organizing your Pinterest boards, including board creation, categorization, and maintenance.

Developing a Content Strategy

Before diving into board organization, it's essential to develop a content strategy that outlines the types of content you'll share on Pinterest. Consider the following content categories for real estate agents:

- Property listings: Showcase your available properties with visually appealing images and informative descriptions.
- Home staging tips: Share advice on how to stage properties for sale or rent, including DIY projects and professional services.

- Neighborhood guides: Create boards that highlight the unique features, amenities, and attractions of the neighborhoods where you operate.
- Real estate infographics: Share informative and visually engaging infographics related to the real estate market, home buying or selling process, or industry trends.
- Testimonials and success stories: Highlight client testimonials and success stories to showcase your expertise and build trust with potential clients.

Creating and Categorizing Boards

Once you've defined your content strategy, create and categorize your boards to reflect the various content types and themes. Consider the following tips:

- Create relevant boards: Develop boards that align with your content strategy and cater to your target audience's interests. Ensure each board has a descriptive title and an informative description containing relevant keywords.
- Use subcategories: Organize your boards into subcategories, if necessary, to help users navigate your content more easily. For example, create separate boards for different property types (e.g., single-family homes, condos, luxury properties) or various home staging tips (e.g., DIY projects, professional staging advice).
- Curate third-party content: Mix in high-quality, relevant content from other Pinterest users to supplement your original content and provide added value to your audience.
- Customize board covers:

Design or select visually appealing and consistent board cover images that represent the content within each board and reinforce your brand identity.

Board Maintenance and Optimization

Maintaining and optimizing your boards is crucial for keeping your Pinterest presence fresh and engaging. Consider the following tips for board maintenance and optimization:

- Regularly update your boards: Add new content to your boards consistently and archive outdated pins to keep your Pinterest presence fresh and relevant.
- Rearrange boards strategically: Place your most popular or seasonally relevant boards at the top of your profile to increase visibility and engagement.
- Monitor board performance: Use Pinterest Analytics to track the performance of your boards, including impressions, clicks, and saves, to identify trends and areas for improvement.
- Optimize boards for search: Include relevant keywords in your board titles and descriptions to improve their discoverability in Pinterest search results.

Organizing your Pinterest boards effectively is essential for creating a user-friendly, engaging, and informative experience for your audience. By developing a content strategy, creating and categorizing relevant boards, and maintaining and optimizing your boards over time, you can build a strong Pinterest presence that generates leads, drives traffic, and positions you as an authority in the real estate industry.

Stay committed to refining your board organization and content strategy based on audience preferences, industry trends, and performance data to ensure the ongoing success of your Pinterest marketing efforts.

CHAPTER 25:

COLLABORATING WITH OTHER USERS

Collaboration is a powerful aspect of Pinterest that allows real estate agents to expand their reach, build relationships, and increase engagement on the platform. In this chapter, we will explore effective strategies for collaborating with other Pinterest users, including joining and creating group boards, partnering with influencers, and engaging with your audience.

Joining and Creating Group Boards

Group boards are a popular way to collaborate with other Pinterest users and share content with a broader audience. Consider the following tips for joining and creating group boards:

- Find relevant group boards: Search for group boards within your niche or local community by using keywords related to your industry or location.
- Request to Join: Once you've identified relevant group boards, follow the board owner and request to join, either by messaging them or following any provided instructions

- Create your group board: If you can't find a suitable group board, consider creating your own. Invite other real estate agents, influencers, or local businesses to collaborate and contribute content.
- Set clear guidelines: Establish guidelines for your group board, including content types, pin frequency, and quality standards, to ensure a cohesive and valuable experience for your audience.

Partnering with Influencers

Influencers can help you reach new audiences and amplify your message on Pinterest. Consider the following tips for partnering with influencers:

1. Identify relevant influencers: Look for influencers within your niche or local community who align with your brand values and have a strong following on Pinterest.
2. Build relationships: Engage with influencers by following them, liking their content, and leaving thoughtful comments to build rapport before proposing a collaboration.
3. Propose a collaboration: Reach out to influencers with a personalized message outlining your collaboration idea, such as co-hosting a webinar, creating a joint Pinterest board, or featuring their content on your profile.
4. Offer value: Ensure your collaboration proposal benefits both parties by offering value to the influencer, such as cross-promotion or access to exclusive resources

Engaging with Your Audience

Building relationships with your audience on Pinterest is essential for fostering trust, loyalty, and engagement. Consider the following tips for engaging with your audience:

1. Respond to comments: Make an effort to respond to comments on your pins and messages from your followers in a timely and thoughtful manner.
2. Ask for feedback: Encourage your audience to share their thoughts, preferences, and questions by asking for feedback on your content or services.
3. Share user-generated content: Feature content created by your audience, such as testimonials or property photos, to show appreciation and foster a sense of community.
4. Organize contests and giveaways: Host contests and giveaways to reward your audience, generate buzz, and encourage user-generated content.

Collaborating with other Pinterest users is a powerful way to expand your reach, build relationships, and increase engagement on the platform. By joining and creating group boards, partnering with influencers, and engaging with your audience, you can create a vibrant and dynamic Pinterest presence that generates leads, drives traffic, and positions you as an authority in the real estate industry. Stay committed to fostering connections and collaborations on Pinterest, adapting your strategies based on audience preferences, industry trends, and performance data to ensure the ongoing success of your Pinterest marketing efforts.

CHAPTER 26:

UTILIZING PINTEREST ADVERTISING OPTIONS

Pinterest offers a range of advertising options for real estate agents looking to boost their visibility, reach new audiences, and generate leads. In this chapter, we will explore the various Pinterest advertising options, including Promoted Pins, Promoted Video Pins, and Carousel Ads, as well as best practices for creating and optimizing your Pinterest ad campaigns.

Pinterest Advertising Options

Pinterest offers several ad formats to help you achieve your marketing objectives:

- Promoted Pins: These are regular pins that you pay to promote, ensuring they appear in front of your target audience in their home feed or search results.
- Promoted Video Pins: Similar to Promoted Pins, these are video pins that you pay to promote, allowing you to share engaging video content with your target audience.

- Carousel Ads: Carousel Ads enable you to showcase multiple images or videos within a single ad, allowing users to swipe through multiple property listings or content pieces.

Creating an Effective Pinterest Ad Campaign

To create a successful Pinterest ad campaign, follow these steps:

- Define your campaign objectives: Determine your advertising goals, such as increasing brand awareness, driving website traffic, or generating leads.
- Choose your ad format: Select the most appropriate ad format based on your objectives and content strategy.
- Target your audience: Use Pinterest's targeting options to reach your desired audience, such as by demographics, interests, or keywords.
- Set your budget and bid: Establish a daily or lifetime budget for your campaign and choose a bidding strategy, such as cost-per-click (CPC) or cost-per-thousand impressions (CPM).
- Design visually appealing ads: Create eye-catching and high-quality ad creatives that align with your brand identity and resonate with your target audience.
- Write compelling ad copy: Craft engaging and informative ad copy that clearly communicates your value proposition and includes a clear call-to-action (CTA).

Optimizing Your Pinterest Ad Campaigns

To ensure the ongoing success of your Pinterest ad campaigns, consider the following optimization tips:

1. Monitor campaign performance: Use Pinterest Ads Manager to track key performance indicators (KPIs) such as impressions, clicks, and conversions to identify trends and areas for improvement.
2. Test different ad creatives: Experiment with various ad designs, copy, and formats to identify which resonate best with your target audience.
3. Adjust targeting and bidding: Continuously refine your audience targeting and bidding strategies based on performance data and insights.
4. Optimize ad scheduling: Analyze when your audience is most active on Pinterest and schedule your ads accordingly to maximize engagement.
5. Implement conversion tracking: Set up Pinterest's conversion tracking to measure the effectiveness of your campaigns and optimize them for better results.

Utilizing Pinterest advertising options can help real estate agents amplify their message, reach new audiences, and generate leads. By understanding the various ad formats, creating effective ad campaigns, and continuously optimizing your efforts based on performance data and insights, you can harness the full potential of Pinterest advertising to drive results for your real estate business.

Stay committed to refining your advertising strategies and adapting to changes in the Pinterest advertising landscape to ensure the ongoing success of your Pinterest marketing efforts

CHAPTER 27:

TIKTOK FOR REAL ESTATE AGENTS

TikTok has rapidly become one of the most popular social media platforms, offering real estate agents a unique opportunity to reach and engage with a broad and diverse audience. In this chapter, we will explore the basics of TikTok, its potential benefits for real estate agents, and how to effectively create and share content on the platform to build your brand and generate leads.

Understanding TikTok

TikTok is a short-form video platform where users can create, edit, and share 15-60 second videos with a wide range of filters, effects, and music. The platform's algorithm is designed to showcase content that is engaging, entertaining, and relevant to users, making it an ideal platform for real estate agents looking to showcase their personality, expertise, and listings in a creative and dynamic way.

Benefits of TikTok for Real Estate Agents

TikTok offers several benefits for real estate agents, including:

1. Access to a large and diverse audience: With millions of active users, TikTok provides real estate agents with the opportunity to reach a wide range of potential clients.
2. High engagement potential: TikTok's short-form video format encourages high levels of user engagement, making it easier for your content to gain traction and visibility.
3. Showcase your personality and expertise: TikTok allows you to share your unique perspective and insights in a fun and engaging way, helping you stand out from the competition and build trust with your audience.
4. Drive website traffic and generate leads: By including links to your website or listings in your profile and video captions, you can drive traffic and generate leads from your TikTok content.

Creating Engaging TikTok Content

To create engaging content on TikTok, consider the following tips:

- Plan your content strategy: Develop a content plan that balances property showcases, real estate tips, and personal insights to keep your audience engaged and informed.
- Embrace creativity: TikTok encourages creativity and experimentation, so don't be afraid to try new formats, effects, and trends to make your content stand out.
- Keep it authentic: Showcase your personality and unique perspective in your videos, as authenticity resonates with TikTok users and helps to build trust.

- Optimize for short attention spans: Keep your videos concise, engaging, and visually appealing to capture and maintain your audience's attention.
- Use hashtags strategically: Include relevant hashtags in your captions to increase the visibility of your content and reach a wider audience.

Growing Your TikTok Following

To grow your following on TikTok, consider the following strategies:

1. Post consistently: Maintain a consistent posting schedule to keep your audience engaged and encourage algorithm-driven growth.
2. Engage with your audience: Respond to comments and messages, and engage with your followers' content to build relationships and foster community.
3. Collaborate with other users: Partner with other real estate agents, influencers, or local businesses to create joint content and expand your reach.
4. Participate in challenges and trends: Join in on popular TikTok challenges and trends relevant to your niche to increase your visibility and attract new followers.
5. Cross-promote on other platforms: Share your TikTok content on other social media platforms and encourage your existing followers to join you on TikTok.

TikTok offers a unique and powerful opportunity for real estate agents to reach and engage with a diverse audience through creative and entertaining short-form video content. By understanding the platform's dynamics, creating engaging content, and employing effective growth strategies, you can leverage TikTok to build your brand, showcase your expertise, and generate leads for your real estate business. Stay committed to refining your TikTok content strategy and adapting to the platform's ever-evolving trends and features to ensure the ongoing success of your TikTok marketing efforts. With consistency, creativity, and authenticity, you can make the most of TikTok as a powerful tool for growing your real estate business.

CHAPTER 28:

SETTING UP A PROFILE

Creating a strong and professional TikTok profile is essential for real estate agents looking to build their brand and attract potential clients on the platform. In this chapter, we will guide you through the process of setting up a TikTok profile, optimizing it for maximum impact, and making it stand out to attract followers and generate leads.

Creating Your TikTok Account

To create your TikTok account, follow these steps:

- Download the TikTok app: Download the TikTok app from the App Store or Google Play Store on your smartphone or tablet.
- Sign up for an account: Open the app and tap on the "Sign up" or "Profile" icon, then follow the prompts to sign up using your preferred method, such as your email, phone number, or a social media account.

- Switch to a Pro Account: Once you've created your account, go to your profile, tap on the three-dot icon in the top-right corner, and select "Manage account." From there, tap on "Switch to Pro Account" and choose "Business" as your account type. This will unlock additional features and analytics, which can be helpful for real estate agents.

Optimizing Your TikTok Profile

To optimize your TikTok profile, consider the following tips:
1. Choose a professional username: Select a username that reflects your real estate business or personal brand, making it easy for users to find and recognize you.
2. Upload a high-quality profile picture: Use a professional, high-resolution headshot or your business logo as your profile picture to make a strong first impression.
3. Craft a compelling bio: Write a brief but informative bio that highlights your expertise, experience, and unique value proposition as a real estate agent. Include relevant keywords to make your profile more discoverable, and don't forget to add a touch of personality.
4. Add your website and contact information: Include a link to your website or a specific landing page in your profile to drive traffic and generate leads. You can also add your email address and phone number to make it easy for potential clients to get in touch with you.
5. Connect your other social media accounts: Link your TikTok account to your other social media profiles, such as Instagram, Facebook, and YouTube, to cross-promote your content and expand your reach.

Consistency in Visual Identity

Maintain a consistent visual identity across your TikTok profile and content by using the same color schemes, fonts, and design elements as your other marketing materials. This will help to establish a cohesive brand image and make your content more recognizable to your audience.

Regularly Update Your Profile

Periodically review and update your TikTok profile to ensure it accurately reflects your current real estate business, expertise, and offerings. Keep your profile fresh and up-to-date to maintain credibility and trust with your audience.

Setting up and optimizing a professional TikTok profile is crucial for real estate agents looking to leverage the platform to build their brand, engage with potential clients, and generate leads. By creating a visually appealing, informative, and cohesive profile, you can establish a strong presence on TikTok and set the foundation for a successful content strategy. Stay committed to maintaining a polished and current profile that accurately represents your real estate business and expertise, and you will be well on your way to harnessing the power of TikTok in your marketing efforts.

CHAPTER 29:

CREATING AND EDITING VIDEOS

Creating engaging, high-quality TikTok videos is essential for real estate agents looking to build their brand and connect with potential clients on the platform. In this chapter, we will provide a comprehensive guide to creating and editing TikTok videos, covering everything from planning and filming to editing and optimizing your content for maximum impact.

Planning Your TikTok Videos

Before you start filming, take the time to plan your TikTok video content. Consider the following tips when planning your videos:

- Define your goals: Determine the purpose of your video, whether it's showcasing a property, sharing real estate tips, or providing a behind-the-scenes look at your daily work.
- Research trends and hashtags: Keep an eye on TikTok trends and popular hashtags within the real estate niche, and consider incorporating them into your content to increase visibility and engagement.

- Develop a storyboard: Outline the key scenes and elements of your video, ensuring it has a clear structure and narrative.
- Prepare your script: Write a script for your video, including any dialogue, voiceover, or captions you plan to use.

Filming Your TikTok Videos

When it comes to filming your TikTok videos, consider the following best practices:

- Choose the right equipment: Invest in a smartphone with a high-quality camera, a tripod or stabilizer, and a microphone to ensure your videos look and sound professional.
- Select a suitable location: Choose a well-lit, clutter-free location for your video, ensuring it aligns with your content's purpose and showcases the property or subject matter effectively.
- Frame your shots: Use the rule of thirds and other composition techniques to frame your shots, creating visually appealing and dynamic content.
- Film multiple takes: Record multiple takes of each scene to give yourself options during the editing process.
- Use TikTok's built-in tools: Familiarize yourself with TikTok's in-app filming and editing tools, such as filters, effects, and timers, to enhance your content and streamline the production process.

Editing Your TikTok Videos

Once you've filmed your content, it's time to edit your video. Here are some tips for editing your TikTok videos:

1. Choose an editing app: There are several video editing apps available, both within TikTok and externally, such as InShot, Adobe Premiere Rush, and VivaVideo. Select the app that best suits your needs and skill level.
2. Trim and arrange clips: Review your footage and trim any unnecessary or repetitive sections, arranging your clips in a logical and engaging order.
3. Add transitions and effects: Use transitions and effects to create a seamless and visually appealing video. Be mindful not to overdo it, as too many effects can detract from your content's message.
4. Incorporate text and captions: Add text, captions, or subtitles to your video to provide context and make it accessible to a wider audience.
5. Include music or voiceover: Add music, sound effects, or voiceover to your video, ensuring it complements your content and adheres to TikTok's copyright guidelines.

Optimizing Your TikTok Videos

To maximize the impact of your TikTok videos, consider the following optimization tips:

- Choose a captivating thumbnail: Select a visually appealing and relevant thumbnail to entice users to watch your video.

- Craft an engaging caption: Write a concise and engaging caption that provides context and encourages users to interact with your content.
- Use hashtags strategically: Include relevant and trending hashtags in your caption to increase your video's visibility and reach a wider audience.
- Post at optimal times: Research the best times to post on TikTok for your target audience, taking into account factors such as location, demographics, and platform usage patterns.
- Engage with your audience: Respond to comments, questions, and messages from your viewers to foster engagement and build relationships with your audience.

Analyzing Your TikTok Video Performance

Track the performance of your TikTok videos using the platform's analytics tools, available through your Pro Account. Analyze metrics such as views, likes, comments, shares, and watch time to gain insights into your content's performance and your audience's preferences.

- Identify trends and patterns: Look for patterns in your video performance to determine what types of content resonate best with your audience.
- Adjust your content strategy: Based on your video performance analysis, adjust your content strategy to focus on creating more of the types of videos that perform well, while refining or eliminating less successful content.

- Set measurable goals: Establish specific, measurable goals for your TikTok video performance, such as increasing views, engagement, or followers, and track your progress over time.

Creating and editing compelling TikTok videos is an essential skill for real estate agents looking to harness the platform's potential for building their brand, engaging with potential clients, and generating leads. By planning your content, filming high-quality footage, editing your videos effectively, and optimizing them for maximum impact, you can create a strong presence on TikTok and attract a loyal and engaged audience. Continuously analyze your video performance, refine your content strategy, and stay up to date with TikTok trends and best practices to ensure ongoing success in your video marketing efforts.

CHAPTER 30:

LEVERAGING POPULAR TRENDS

TikTok trends play a crucial role in the platform's dynamic and engaging atmosphere. By leveraging these trends, real estate agents can create content that resonates with their audience and increases their visibility on the platform. In this chapter, we will discuss how to identify and utilize popular TikTok trends, adapt them to your real estate niche, and create captivating content that captures your audience's attention.

Identifying Popular TikTok Trends

To stay up-to-date with the latest TikTok trends, consider the following strategies:

- Monitor the "For You" page: The "For You" page is TikTok's main feed, showcasing a curated selection of trending content based on user preferences. Regularly check this feed to identify trends that resonate with your target audience.

- Follow relevant hashtags: Keep track of hashtags related to real estate and your niche to discover trending content within your industry.
- Connect with industry influencers: Follow and engage with other real estate agents, industry influencers, and content creators on TikTok to stay informed about current trends and best practices.
- Use TikTok's Discover tab: The Discover tab allows you to search for trending hashtags, challenges, and content related to specific topics or industries.
- Stay informed through external sources: Follow industry blogs, social media accounts, and news outlets to stay updated on TikTok trends and platform updates.

Adapting Trends to Your Real Estate Niche

When leveraging popular TikTok trends, it's essential to adapt them to your real estate niche to ensure your content remains relevant and valuable to your audience. Here are some tips for adapting trends to your niche:

- Align trends with your brand and objectives: Choose trends that align with your brand's personality, values, and marketing objectives. Avoid trends that may be inappropriate, off-brand, or unrelated to your real estate business.
- Showcase your expertise: Use trends as an opportunity to demonstrate your industry knowledge, expertise, and unique value proposition as a real estate agent.

- Highlight properties and communities: Adapt trends to showcase your properties, local communities, and real estate-related content in a creative and engaging manner.
- Tell a story: Use trending formats, such as challenges or storytelling techniques, to share your real estate journey, client experiences, or success stories.

Creating Content Based on TikTok Trends

Once you've identified and adapted a trend to your real estate niche, follow these steps to create your content:

- Plan your video: Develop a storyboard and script based on the trend, incorporating your unique real estate angle and message.
- Film your video: Record your video using high-quality equipment, ensuring it aligns with the trend's format and style while showcasing your real estate content effectively.
- Edit your video: Use TikTok's in-app editing tools or external video editing software to trim, arrange, and enhance your footage, adding effects, transitions, text, and music as needed.
- Optimize your video: Craft an engaging caption, select a captivating thumbnail, and include relevant hashtags to increase your video's visibility and reach.
- Engage with your audience: Respond to comments and messages from your viewers, and participate in conversations around the trend to build relationships and foster engagement.

Monitoring the Performance of Trend-Based Content

Track the performance of your trend-based content using TikTok's analytics tools to gain insights into its effectiveness and your audience's preferences. Use this information to refine your content strategy, focusing on trends that resonate with your audience and generate the best results.

Leveraging popular TikTok trends is an effective way for real estate agents to create engaging content, reach a wider audience, and stay relevant on the platform. By identifying and adapting trends to your real estate niche, you can develop captivating content that resonates with your target audience and showcases your expertise as a real estate agent.

Staying up-to-date with TikTok trends requires consistent monitoring of the platform, engaging with industry influencers, and staying informed through external sources. As you incorporate trends into your content strategy, it's essential to maintain your unique brand voice and remain authentic to your real estate business.

Remember to analyze the performance of your trend-based content to identify what works best for your audience and refine your content strategy accordingly. By leveraging TikTok trends effectively and creatively, you can grow your online presence, build your brand, and ultimately generate more leads and opportunities for your real estate business.

CHAPTER 31:

ENGAGING WITH THE TIKTOK COMMUNITY

Engaging with the TikTok community is crucial for real estate agents looking to build their brand, establish credibility, and create meaningful connections with potential clients. Active participation in the community not only helps you stay informed about the latest trends and best practices but also fosters trust, loyalty, and a sense of camaraderie among your followers. In this chapter, we will discuss strategies for effectively engaging with the TikTok community, including commenting, direct messaging, collaborating, and participating in challenges and events.

Commenting on TikTok

Commenting on other users' content is a valuable way to engage with the TikTok community. Here are some tips for leaving thoughtful and engaging comments:

- Be genuine: Write authentic, meaningful comments that contribute to the conversation and demonstrate your interest in the content.

- Be supportive and positive: Encourage and uplift other creators by sharing positive feedback and expressing appreciation for their content.
- Ask questions: Engage in conversation by asking relevant questions or sharing your thoughts on the topic.
- Respond to comments on your content: Make an effort to reply to comments on your videos, answer questions, and engage in conversation with your audience.

Direct Messaging on TikTok

Direct messaging allows you to engage in one-on-one conversations with other TikTok users. Use direct messages to:

1. Network with industry professionals: Connect with other real estate agents, industry influencers, and content creators to share ideas, insights, and collaborate.
2. Build relationships with potential clients: Respond to inquiries, provide additional information about your services, and answer questions from potential clients.
3. Share exclusive content: Send personalized video messages, updates, or behind-the-scenes content to your most engaged followers to strengthen your connection with them.

Collaborating with Other Creators

Collaboration with other TikTok creators can lead to increased visibility, audience growth, and new opportunities. Here are some tips for successful collaborations:

1. Identify potential collaborators: Look for TikTok users with a similar target audience, complementary expertise, or shared interests in the real estate industry.
2. Develop a collaboration concept: Brainstorm ideas for a collaboration that will provide value to both your audiences and showcase your combined expertise.
3. Communicate effectively: Establish clear communication channels, share ideas openly, and be respectful and professional throughout the collaboration process.
4. Promote the collaboration: Share your collaborative content on your TikTok profile, as well as on other social media platforms, and encourage your audience to engage with and share the content.

Participating in Challenges and Events

Joining TikTok challenges and events can help you connect with the community, showcase your creativity, and increase your visibility on the platform. Here's how to participate effectively:

1. Choose relevant challenges and events: Select challenges and events that align with your real estate niche, brand values, and marketing objectives.
2. Adapt the challenge to your content: Customize the challenge or event to incorporate your unique real estate angle, providing value and relevance to your audience.
3. Promote your participation: Share your challenge or event participation on TikTok and other social media platforms, and engage with other participants to build connections and foster a sense of community.

Engaging with the TikTok community is essential for real estate agents looking to build their brand and create meaningful connections on the platform. By actively participating in conversations, collaborating with other creators, and joining challenges and events, you can foster trust, loyalty, and a sense of camaraderie among your followers. In doing so, you will not only enhance your online presence but also establish yourself as an approachable, knowledgeable, and credible real estate agent. As you continue to engage with the TikTok community, remember to maintain your unique brand voice and remain authentic in your interactions, as this will resonate with your audience and help you build lasting connections with potential clients.

CHAPTER 32:

INSTAGRAM FOR REAL ESTATE AGENTS

Instagram is an incredibly powerful platform for real estate agents, offering a visually-driven experience that allows you to showcase properties, share valuable content, and connect with your target audience. With its various features, such as Instagram Stories, IGTV, and Reels, you can create a comprehensive content strategy that builds your brand and generates leads. In this chapter, we will discuss the benefits of using Instagram for your real estate business, setting up an optimized profile, and creating engaging content to grow your audience.

Benefits of Instagram for Real Estate Agents

Using Instagram for your real estate business offers numerous benefits, including:
- Visual storytelling: Instagram's focus on visual content allows you to showcase stunning property photos and videos, providing an immersive experience for potential clients.

- Engagement opportunities: Instagram's interactive features, such as Stories, polls, and Q&As, enable you to connect with your audience on a more personal level.
- Content variety: With Instagram's multiple content formats, you can create a diverse content strategy that caters to different user preferences and consumption habits.
- Increased reach: Instagram's algorithm and discoverability features, such as the Explore page and hashtags, can help increase your content's visibility and reach a broader audience.
- Networking and collaboration: Instagram provides ample opportunities to network with other real estate professionals, industry influencers, and potential clients, facilitating collaboration and knowledge sharing.

Setting Up an Optimized Instagram Profile

To create a professional and effective Instagram profile, follow these steps:

1. Choose an appropriate username: Select a username that reflects your real estate brand and is easy to remember.
2. Create a professional profile picture: Use a high-quality, professional headshot that conveys your personality and aligns with your brand image.
3. Write a compelling bio: Craft a concise, informative bio that highlights your expertise, unique selling points, and contact information. Use emojis, line breaks, and a clear call-to-action to make your bio visually appealing and easy to read.

- Convert to a business profile: Switch to a business profile to access additional features, such as analytics, advertising options, and the ability to add contact information.
- Connect your other social media accounts: Link your Instagram profile to your Facebook, Twitter, and other social media accounts to cross-promote your content and facilitate seamless sharing.

Creating Engaging Instagram Content

To create engaging Instagram content that resonates with your audience, consider the following tips:

1. Showcase properties: Share visually stunning images and videos of your property listings, highlighting unique features and offering virtual tours.
2. Share valuable information: Post infographics, market updates, and educational content to demonstrate your expertise and provide value to your audience.
3. Tell stories: Use Instagram Stories, Reels, and IGTV to share behind-the-scenes glimpses, client testimonials, and your personal real estate journey.
4. Utilize hashtags strategically: Research and use relevant hashtags to increase your content's visibility and reach a larger audience.
5. Maintain a consistent aesthetic: Develop a consistent visual style for your feed, using a cohesive color palette, filters, and editing techniques to create a visually appealing and recognizable brand identity.

Engaging with Your Instagram Audience

Building relationships and engaging with your audience is crucial for your Instagram success. Follow these strategies to foster meaningful connections:

1. Respond to comments and messages: Make an effort to reply to comments on your posts, answer questions, and engage in conversations with your followers.
2. Collaborate with industry influencers: Partner with influencers and other real estate professionals to create collaborative content, host giveaways, or conduct takeovers on each other's accounts.
3. Participate in Instagram challenges and events: Join relevant challenges, events, or community initiatives to connect with other users, showcase your creativity, and increase your visibility.
4. Share user-generated content: Encourage your clients and followers to share their experiences with your services, and repost their content on your feed or Stories, giving them credit for their contribution.
5. Analyze and adapt: Use Instagram analytics to track your content's performance, identify trends, and adjust your content strategy accordingly to better engage your audience.

Leveraging Instagram Advertising

To increase your reach and visibility on Instagram, consider utilizing its advertising options:

1. Sponsored posts: Boost your most engaging content with sponsored posts that target specific audience segments based on demographics, interests, and behaviors.
2. Story ads: Create immersive, full-screen ads in the Stories format to capture your audience's attention and encourage them to learn more about your real estate services.
3. Carousel ads: Use carousel ads to showcase multiple images or videos in a single ad, allowing you to feature several properties or highlight different aspects of a single property.
4. IGTV and Reels ads: Experiment with ads in IGTV and Reels formats to reach users consuming long-form or short-form video content.
5. Track and optimize: Monitor the performance of your ads, test different creatives and targeting options, and optimize your campaigns to maximize your return on investment.

Instagram offers real estate agents a powerful platform to showcase properties, share valuable content, and connect with their target audience. By optimizing your profile, creating engaging content, and actively participating in the community, you can build your brand, generate leads, and grow your real estate business. Remember to analyze your performance, adapt your strategy, and stay up-to-date with Instagram's latest features and trends to ensure continued success on the platform.

CHAPTER 33:

OPTIMIZING YOUR PROFILE

A well-optimized Instagram profile is essential for creating a strong online presence and attracting potential clients in the real estate industry. In this chapter, we will discuss various aspects of optimizing your Instagram profile, including username selection, profile picture, bio, contact information, highlights, and linking to your other online properties.

Choosing the Right Username

Your Instagram username should reflect your real estate brand and be easily recognizable. Keep the following tips in mind when choosing your username:

- Keep it simple and memorable: Choose a username that is easy to remember and type.
- Avoid special characters or numbers: Try to avoid using special characters or numbers, as they can make your username harder to find and remember

- Align with your other social media handles: Ideally, use the same or similar username across all your social media platforms to maintain consistency and make it easier for your audience to find you.

Selecting a Professional Profile Picture

Your profile picture should create a positive first impression and convey your brand's identity. Consider the following tips for choosing an appropriate profile picture:

1. Use a high-quality headshot: A professional, high-resolution headshot will help convey your expertise and trustworthiness.
2. Be consistent across platforms: Use the same profile picture on all your social media accounts to maintain a consistent brand image.
3. Keep it updated: Regularly update your profile picture to ensure it accurately represents your current appearance.

Crafting a Compelling Bio

Your Instagram bio should provide a concise yet informative overview of your real estate services, unique selling points, and contact information. To create a compelling bio, follow these guidelines:

- Communicate your expertise: Clearly state your profession, specialization, and any certifications or awards you've received.

- Add personality: Inject some personality into your bio by sharing your interests, values, or a personal motto.
- Include contact information: Make it easy for potential clients to get in touch by providing your email address, phone number, or a link to your website.
- Use emojis and line breaks: Emojis and line breaks can help make your bio visually appealing and easy to read.
- Add a call-to-action: Encourage users to take action, such as visiting your website, signing up for your newsletter, or contacting you for a consultation.

Adding Contact Information and Call-to-Action Buttons

A business profile on Instagram allows you to add contact information and call-to-action buttons to your profile. To add these features, follow these steps:

1. Convert your profile to a business profile: If you haven't already, switch to a business profile to access additional features, such as contact information and call-to-action buttons.
2. Add contact information: Provide your email address, phone number, and physical address to make it easy for potential clients to reach you.
3. Choose call-to-action buttons: Select the most relevant call-to-action buttons for your business, such as "Call," "Email," "Book Appointment," or "Visit Website."

Creating and Organizing Instagram Highlights
Instagram Highlights are a useful feature for showcasing your most important content directly on your profile. To create and organize Highlights, follow these steps:

1. Select content for Highlights: Choose Stories that best represent your real estate services, such as property tours, client testimonials, and educational content.
2. Create custom Highlight covers: Design visually appealing covers for your Highlights that align with your brand's visual identity.
3. Organize Highlights by category: Arrange your Highlights into categories, such as "Listings," "Tips," "Testimonials," and "Events," to make it easy for your audience to find relevant content.

Linking to Your Other Online Properties

Maximize your online presence by linking your Instagram profile to your other online properties, such as your website, blog, and other social media accounts. To do this, consider the following:

- Include your website link in your bio: Provide a link to your website or blog in your Instagram bio, making it easy for potential clients to learn more about your services.
- Use a link management tool: Platforms like Linktree or bio.fm allow you to create a custom landing page with multiple links, directing users to various online properties, such as your listings, blog posts, and other social media profiles.

- Cross-promote your social media accounts: Occasionally mention your other social media accounts in your Instagram posts and Stories, encouraging your audience to follow you on multiple platforms.

Optimizing Your Profile for Search

Ensure that your Instagram profile is easily discoverable by optimizing it for search. To improve your profile's visibility in search results, follow these tips:

1. Include relevant keywords: Incorporate industry-related keywords in your username and bio to improve your chances of appearing in search results when users look for real estate content.
2. Engage with your audience: Regularly interact with your followers and other users in the real estate community by commenting, liking, and sharing their content. This can help increase your profile's visibility and attract more followers.
3. Leverage hashtags: Use relevant and popular hashtags in your posts to increase their discoverability in search results and attract potential clients.

Optimizing your Instagram profile is crucial for establishing a strong online presence and attracting potential clients in the real estate industry. By carefully selecting your username, profile picture, and crafting a compelling bio, you can effectively communicate your expertise and unique selling points. Additionally, adding contact information, organizing Highlights, and linking to your other online properties can help provide a seamless experience for your audience.

Finally, optimizing your profile for search can ensure that you are easily discoverable by potential clients and other industry professionals, ultimately helping you grow your real estate business.

CHAPTER 34:

CREATING COMPELLING CONTENT

Creating compelling content on Instagram is essential for attracting and engaging your target audience, showcasing your real estate expertise, and ultimately generating leads for your business. In this chapter, we will discuss various content types and strategies for creating engaging Instagram content, including property showcases, behind-the-scenes insights, educational content, user-generated content, and interactive Stories.

Property Showcases

Highlighting properties is a crucial aspect of your Instagram content strategy. Use a mix of visually appealing images and videos to showcase your listings effectively. Consider the following tips:

- Use high-quality images: Share professional, high-resolution images that highlight the best features of each property.

- Create engaging property tours: Produce video tours that give viewers a comprehensive and immersive walkthrough of each property.
- Highlight unique features: Focus on the unique selling points of each property, such as architectural details, amenities, or stunning views.
- Show before-and-after transformations: Share the progress of property renovations or staging to demonstrate your expertise and attention to detail.

Behind-the-Scenes Insights

Giving your audience a glimpse into your daily work life can help humanize your brand and build trust. Share behind-the-scenes content that showcases your personality and work ethic, such as:

1. Daily routines and rituals: Share your morning routine, workout regimen, or a favorite coffee spot to connect with your audience on a personal level.
2. Office and team culture: Showcase your office environment, team-building activities, or company milestones to demonstrate your commitment to a positive work culture.
3. Client interactions: Highlight your interactions with clients, such as consultations, property showings, or negotiation meetings, while maintaining privacy and confidentiality.
4. Industry events: Document your participation in industry conferences, workshops, or networking events to demonstrate your commitment to professional growth.

Educational Content

Educating your audience about real estate topics positions you as an expert in your field and provides value to potential clients. Consider sharing:

1. Real estate tips and advice: Share practical tips for buying, selling, or investing in real estate.
2. Market updates and trends: Provide updates on local market trends, interest rates, or other industry news.
3. Home improvement ideas: Offer suggestions for home renovations, staging, or design that can increase property value or appeal.
4. FAQs: Address frequently asked questions from your clients or followers, either through posts or Instagram Stories.

User-Generated Content

Encourage your clients and followers to share their experiences with your services and repost their content with proper credit. User-generated content can include:

1. Client testimonials: Share written or video testimonials from satisfied clients to build credibility and trust.
2. Property success stories: Highlight the successful sale or purchase of a property and the positive impact it had on your clients.
3. Community involvement: Showcase your clients' participation in local events, charity initiatives, or neighborhood activities.

Interactive Stories

Leverage Instagram Stories to engage with your audience and encourage interaction. Some interactive content ideas include:

1. Polls and quizzes: Use the poll and quiz features to gauge your audience's opinions, preferences, or knowledge of real estate topics.
2. Q&A sessions: Host live or pre-recorded Q&A sessions to answer your followers' questions and provide expert advice.
3. Behind-the-scenes moments: Share candid moments from your daily work life or property showings to connect with your audience on a personal level.
4. Countdowns and announcements: Use the countdown feature to build anticipation for new property listings, open houses, or events.

Creating compelling Instagram content is crucial for attracting and engaging your target audience, showcasing your real estate expertise, and generating leads for your business. By utilizing a diverse mix of content types, such as property showcases, behind-the-scenes insights, educational content, user-generated content, and interactive Stories, you can effectively engage your audience and build your brand on Instagram.

Remember to maintain consistency in your visual identity and brand voice across all content types to ensure a cohesive and recognizable brand image. Additionally, monitor your content's performance using Instagram analytics to identify which types of content resonate most with your audience and adjust your content strategy accordingly.

Ultimately, by producing high-quality, engaging, and value-driven content, you can set yourself apart as a real estate professional and attract potential clients on Instagram. Stay creative, be authentic, and continue to refine your content strategy as you grow your real estate business through the power of social media.

CHAPTER 35:

UTILIZING INSTAGRAM STORIES AND IGTV

Instagram Stories and IGTV are powerful tools for real estate agents to connect with their audience, showcase their expertise, and drive engagement. In this chapter, we will discuss the benefits and best practices for using Instagram Stories and IGTV in your real estate marketing strategy, including content ideas, tips for maximizing engagement, and utilizing Instagram's features to create a seamless user experience.

Instagram Stories

Instagram Stories are short-lived, 15-second photo or video clips that disappear after 24 hours. They offer a more casual and intimate way to engage with your audience, making them perfect for sharing behind-the-scenes content, quick updates, and interactive elements.

Content Ideas for Instagram Stories
- Property sneak peeks: Share exclusive previews of upcoming listings or open houses.

- Behind-the-scenes moments: Show your daily activities, client interactions, or office culture.
- Real estate tips and advice: Offer quick tips, market updates, or industry news.
- Q&A sessions: Answer questions from your audience or address common real estate concerns.
- Polls and quizzes: Engage your audience with interactive polls or quizzes on real estate topics.

Tips for Maximizing Engagement

- Use hashtags and location tags: Increase your Stories' discoverability by including relevant hashtags and location tags.
- Add captions or text overlays: Ensure your content is accessible to all users by adding captions or text overlays to your videos.
- Utilize stickers and GIFs: Enhance your Stories with eye-catching stickers, GIFs, or other creative elements.
- Save and organize Stories into Highlights: Preserve your best Stories by saving them as Highlights on your profile, making it easy for users to find and revisit your content.

IGTV

IGTV is Instagram's platform for sharing long-form video content, allowing you to post videos up to 60 minutes in length. This format is ideal for in-depth property tours, interviews, or educational content that requires more time than a regular Instagram post or Story.

Content Ideas for IGTV

- Comprehensive property tours: Showcase your listings with detailed video walkthroughs.
- Expert interviews: Collaborate with industry professionals, such as mortgage brokers, interior designers, or home inspectors, to provide valuable insights.
- Educational series: Create a series of videos that cover various real estate topics in depth.
- Client testimonials: Share longer-format success stories or in-depth client experiences.

Tips for Maximizing Engagement

- Use a captivating thumbnail: Attract viewers with a visually appealing and relevant thumbnail image.
- Write compelling titles and descriptions: Craft informative and engaging titles and descriptions, incorporating relevant keywords to increase discoverability.
- Promote your IGTV content: Share previews of your IGTV videos on your feed and Stories to drive traffic to your channel.
- Engage with viewers: Respond to comments and engage with your audience to create a sense of community around your content.

Effectively utilizing Instagram Stories and IGTV can significantly enhance your real estate marketing strategy and help you connect with your audience on a deeper level.

By creating diverse, engaging, and value-driven content, you can establish yourself as an industry expert and build trust with your target audience. Stay up-to-date with Instagram's latest features and best practices to continue refining your approach and maximizing your success on the platform.

CHAPTER 36:

ENGAGING WITH YOUR AUDIENCE

Engaging with your Instagram audience is crucial for building relationships, fostering trust, and ultimately converting followers into clients. In this chapter, we will discuss strategies for interacting with your audience, including techniques for responding to comments and messages, collaborating with other users, and creating a sense of community around your real estate brand.

Responding to Comments and Messages

Timely and thoughtful responses to comments and messages are essential for maintaining a strong connection with your audience. Consider the following tips for effective engagement:

- Respond promptly: Show your followers that you value their input by responding to their comments and messages as quickly as possible.
- Be genuine and personable: Use a friendly and conversational tone to establish an authentic connection with your audience

- Provide valuable information: Offer helpful advice, answer questions, and address concerns to position yourself as a knowledgeable resource.
- Encourage further interaction: Ask open-ended questions or seek feedback to keep the conversation going and deepen your connection with your followers.

Collaborating with Other Users

Collaborating with other Instagram users can expand your reach, introduce you to new audiences, and provide additional value to your followers. Consider the following collaboration ideas:

1. Partner with local businesses: Collaborate with local businesses, such as home decor stores, landscaping companies, or moving services, to offer exclusive discounts, co-host events, or create joint content.
2. Conduct interviews: Interview industry professionals, such as mortgage brokers, home inspectors, or interior designers, to provide expert insights and advice to your audience.
3. Share user-generated content: Encourage your clients and followers to share their experiences with your services, and repost their content with proper credit.
4. Participate in industry-related challenges or hashtags: Join trending challenges or use popular real estate hashtags to connect with other professionals and potential clients.

Creating a Sense of Community

Fostering a sense of community around your real estate brand can help you build loyalty, trust, and long-term relationships with your audience.

1. Host virtual events: Organize live Q&A sessions, webinars, or virtual open houses to engage your audience and provide valuable information.
2. Share success stories: Highlight the positive impact your services have had on your clients to demonstrate your commitment to their satisfaction.
3. Recognize and celebrate milestones: Acknowledge your clients' achievements, such as closing on a new home or completing a renovation project, to show your appreciation and support.
4. Encourage interaction among followers: Pose questions, create polls, or share discussion prompts to facilitate conversation and connection among your audience.

Engaging with your Instagram audience is a key component of building a successful real estate brand on the platform. By responding to comments and messages, collaborating with other users, and fostering a sense of community, you can establish strong connections with your followers and position yourself as a trusted resource in the real estate industry. Continue to refine your engagement strategies and stay attuned to your audience's needs to maximize your impact and drive business growth.

CHAPTER 37:

CROSS-PLATFORM STRATEGIES FOR REAL ESTATE AGENTS

A comprehensive social media strategy for real estate agents should involve leveraging multiple platforms to maximize reach, engagement, and conversions. In this chapter, we will explore cross-platform strategies that can help you create a cohesive and consistent brand presence across various social media channels, including content repurposing, cross-promotion, and analytics tracking.

Content Repurposing

Content repurposing involves adapting and reusing content across multiple platforms to maximize its value and reach a broader audience. Consider the following techniques for repurposing your real estate content:

- Transform long-form content: Break down longer pieces, such as blog posts or IGTV videos, into smaller segments that can be shared as Instagram posts, Stories, or Pinterest pins.

- Adapt visuals for different platforms: Modify images or graphics to fit the dimensions and style of each platform, such as creating vertical images for Pinterest or square images for Instagram.
- Convert static content into interactive formats: Turn infographics, blog posts, or articles into engaging videos, quizzes, or polls for increased engagement on platforms like TikTok or Instagram.
- Utilize user-generated content: Share client testimonials, success stories, or property photos across various platforms to showcase your real estate services and build social proof.

Cross-Promotion

Cross-promotion involves promoting your content and activities on one platform through your other social media channels. Use the following cross-promotion strategies to increase your reach and visibility:

- Share platform-specific content previews: Tease upcoming content, such as a YouTube video or IGTV episode, on your other social media channels to drive traffic and encourage followers to engage with your content on multiple platforms.
- Leverage platform-specific features: Utilize features like Instagram's "Swipe Up" functionality in Stories or Pinterest's "Save" button to direct users to your other social media profiles or external content.

- Collaborate with other users: Partner with influencers, industry professionals, or local businesses and cross-promote your collaborations across your social media channels to reach new audiences and increase credibility.
- Encourage followers to connect on multiple platforms: Remind your audience to follow you on other social media channels to stay up-to-date with your latest content and activities.

Analytics Tracking and Reporting

Tracking your performance across multiple platforms is crucial for identifying strengths, weaknesses, and opportunities for growth. Implement the following practices to effectively monitor your cross-platform performance:

1. Utilize platform-specific analytics: Analyze each platform's native analytics tools, such as Instagram Insights, YouTube Analytics, or Facebook Page Insights, to track your performance and identify trends.
2. Set up a unified analytics dashboard: Use third-party tools or create a custom dashboard to consolidate your analytics data from multiple platforms, allowing for easier analysis and comparison.
3. Track key performance indicators (KPIs): Monitor KPIs, such as engagement rates, follower growth, and conversion rates, to evaluate the success of your cross-platform strategies and inform future decision-making.
4. Regularly review and adjust your strategy: Use the insights gained from your analytics data to refine your cross-platform strategy, optimize your content, and improve overall performance.

Implementing effective cross-platform strategies is essential for maximizing the potential of your social media efforts as a real estate agent. By repurposing content, cross-promoting your activities, and tracking your performance across multiple platforms, you can create a cohesive and consistent brand presence that resonates with your target audience and drives business growth. Stay adaptable and responsive to the ever-evolving social media landscape to ensure continued success in the competitive real estate market.

CHAPTER 38:

INTEGRATING YOUR SOCIAL MEDIA EFFORTS

Integrating your social media efforts with your overall marketing and business operations is crucial for creating a seamless and effective real estate brand experience. In this chapter, we will explore strategies for incorporating social media into various aspects of your business, including your website, email marketing, CRM systems, and offline marketing initiatives.

Integrating Social Media with Your Website

Your website is often the first point of contact for potential clients, and integrating your social media presence can help create a cohesive brand experience. Consider these tips for incorporating social media into your website:

- Add social media icons: Include prominent and easily accessible icons linking to your social media profiles on your website's header, footer, or sidebar.

- Embed social media feeds: Display live feeds of your Instagram, Facebook, or Twitter updates on your website to showcase your active presence and encourage website visitors to follow you on social media.
- Share blog posts on social media: Promote your website's blog posts on your social media channels to drive traffic and increase engagement with your content.
- Add social sharing buttons: Enable visitors to easily share your website content, such as blog posts or property listings, on their own social media profiles.

Integrating Social Media with Email Marketing

Email marketing can complement your social media efforts by nurturing leads, increasing engagement, and driving conversions. Implement these strategies to integrate social media with your email marketing campaigns:

- Include social media icons in your email signature and newsletter templates: Make it easy for your email recipients to connect with you on social media by adding links to your profiles.
- Promote social media content in your newsletters: Share highlights from your social media channels, such as popular posts, upcoming events, or exclusive promotions, in your email newsletters.
- Encourage email subscribers to engage on social media: Include calls-to-action inviting your email subscribers to follow, like, or share your content on social media.

- Use email marketing to support social media campaigns: Coordinate your email marketing and social media efforts to promote special events, webinars, or contests.

Integrating Social Media with CRM Systems
Customer relationship management (CRM) systems can help you track and manage your interactions with leads and clients across multiple channels, including social media. Consider these tips for integrating social media with your CRM:

1. Connect your social media accounts: Link your social media profiles to your CRM system to consolidate your interactions and communications in one place.
2. Track social media engagement: Monitor your leads' and clients' engagement with your social media content, such as likes, comments, and shares, to gain insights into their preferences and interests.
3. Set up social listening alerts: Receive notifications in your CRM system when specific keywords or phrases are mentioned on social media, allowing you to identify opportunities for engagement and lead generation.
4. Leverage social data for personalized outreach: Use the information gathered from social media to tailor your communications and offers to your leads' and clients' specific needs and interests.

Integrating Social Media with Offline Marketing Initiatives

Social media can also enhance your offline marketing efforts by extending your reach and reinforcing your brand message. Consider these strategies for integrating social media with your offline marketing initiatives:

1. Include social media icons on print materials: Add your social media handles and icons to business cards, brochures, and other print materials to encourage potential clients to connect with you online.
2. Promote offline events on social media: Create buzz around your open houses, workshops, or community events by sharing updates, photos, and videos on your social media channels.
3. Use QR codes: Add QR codes to your print materials or signage that link to your social media profiles, making it easy for potential clients to follow you with a simple scan.
4. Incorporate social media into presentations: When giving presentations or hosting seminars, include your social media handles, screenshots of your profiles, or examples of successful social media campaigns to showcase your expertise and encourage attendees to follow you.
5. Leverage hashtags for offline events: Create unique hashtags for your offline events, such as open houses or networking gatherings, and encourage attendees to use them when sharing updates or photos on social media. This will create a virtual conversation around your event and help increase your online visibility.
6. Display social media testimonials: Showcase positive reviews and testimonials from your social media profiles in your office or at events to build credibility and trust with potential clients.

Integrating your social media efforts with your overall marketing and business operations is essential for creating a comprehensive and effective real estate brand experience.

By incorporating social media into your website, email marketing, CRM systems, and offline marketing initiatives, you can create a seamless and consistent brand presence that engages potential clients across multiple touchpoints. Stay adaptable and open to new opportunities for integration as the digital landscape continues to evolve, ensuring your real estate business remains at the forefront of industry trends and best practices.

CHAPTER 39:

CROSS-PROMOTION STRATEGIES

Cross-promotion strategies are essential for maximizing the impact of your social media presence and ensuring your content reaches a broader audience. In this chapter, we will explore various methods for promoting your content across different platforms, collaborations with other agents or businesses, and utilizing user-generated content to amplify your message.

Promoting Content Across Platforms

To increase your reach and engagement, consider repurposing and promoting your content across multiple social media platforms. Here are some strategies to effectively cross-promote your content:

- Adapt content for different platforms: Tailor your content to suit the unique features and audiences of each platform. For example, create a short teaser video for Instagram and a longer, more in-depth version for YouTube.

- Schedule coordinated posts: Plan and schedule your content to be shared across platforms simultaneously, ensuring a consistent message and maximizing exposure.
- Link to related content: Encourage followers to engage with your content on other platforms by sharing links to related posts or videos.
- Use platform-specific features: Leverage features unique to each platform, such as Instagram Stories, Twitter polls, or Facebook Events, to promote your content and encourage engagement.

Collaborating with Other Agents and Businesses

Forming strategic partnerships and collaborating with other agents or businesses can help increase your exposure and credibility. Consider these collaboration strategies:

1. Co-host events or webinars: Partner with other agents or businesses to host events or webinars, and promote them across your social media channels.
2. Share each other's content: Agree to share and promote each other's content, such as blog posts, videos, or listings, across your respective social media profiles.
3. Feature guest contributors: Invite other agents or industry experts to contribute guest articles or videos to your blog or YouTube channel, and cross-promote the content on social media.
4. Conduct interviews or Q&A sessions: Host live interviews or Q&A sessions with other agents or industry professionals, and share the recordings across your social media channels.

Utilizing User-Generated Content

User-generated content (UGC) can help amplify your message and increase engagement by involving your audience in your content creation. Implement these strategies to leverage UGC in your cross-promotion efforts:

1. Encourage clients to share their experiences: Ask satisfied clients to share photos, videos, or testimonials of their experiences with your services, and feature their content on your social media profiles.
2. Create a branded hashtag: Develop a unique hashtag for your real estate business and encourage clients or followers to use it when sharing relevant content. Monitor the hashtag and share the best posts on your own profiles.
3. Host contests or challenges: Organize social media contests or challenges that encourage followers to create and share content related to your real estate business. Offer prizes or incentives to increase participation.
4. Feature community content: Share content created by local community members, such as photos of neighborhood events or popular local spots, to showcase your connection to the community and encourage engagement.

Effective cross-promotion strategies are crucial for maximizing the reach and impact of your social media efforts. By promoting content across platforms, collaborating with other agents or businesses, and utilizing user-generated content, you can ensure your message reaches a wider audience and drives increased engagement.

Stay flexible and open to new cross-promotion opportunities as the social media landscape evolves, keeping your real estate business at the forefront of industry trends and best practices.

CHAPTER 40:

CONTENT REPURPOSING

Content repurposing is the process of taking existing content and transforming it into various formats or for different platforms. This strategy allows you to extend the life of your content, maximize its reach, and engage with your audience on multiple channels. In this chapter, we will explore various methods for repurposing your existing content for maximum impact and efficiency.

Benefits of Content Repurposing

Repurposing your content offers several benefits:

- Expand your reach: By adapting your content for different platforms and formats, you can connect with a wider audience and increase your visibility.
- Improve your SEO: Creating multiple versions of your content can help improve your search engine rankings, as search engines value fresh and diverse content.

- Save time and resources: Repurposing existing content is more efficient than creating entirely new content from scratch, allowing you to maintain a consistent content schedule without overextending your resources.
- Reinforce your message: Repetition helps build brand awareness and solidify your message in the minds of your audience. Repurposing content allows you to reiterate your key points in various formats, making it more memorable and effective.

Strategies for Content Repurposing

Here are some strategies to repurpose your existing content:

- Turn blog posts into videos or vice versa: Transform written content from blog posts into video format or adapt video content into a written format. This allows you to engage with your audience through different mediums and cater to their content consumption preferences.
- Create infographics or slideshows: Summarize your long-form content, such as blog posts or reports, into visually appealing infographics or slideshows. These formats are easily shareable on platforms like Pinterest or LinkedIn.
- Develop a podcast or audio content: Convert your blog posts, articles, or video content into audio format, such as a podcast or audiogram. This provides an alternative way for your audience to consume your content, especially when they are on the go.
- Break down long-form content into smaller pieces: Divide lengthy articles, videos, or webinars into shorter, bite-sized content that can be shared across social media platforms.

- Combine multiple pieces of content into a larger resource: Compile related blog posts, articles, or videos into an eBook, guide, or video series. This creates a more comprehensive resource for your audience and adds value to your content library.
- Update and refresh older content: Revisit your older content and update it with new information, data, or insights. This can help maintain the relevance and value of your content while saving time and resources.

Best Practices for Content Repurposing

To effectively repurpose your content, follow these best practices:

1. Ensure content remains relevant and valuable: When repurposing content, make sure it still provides value to your audience and aligns with your brand message.
2. Tailor content to the platform and audience: Adapt your content to suit the unique features and preferences of each platform and its audience.
3. Maintain a consistent brand voice and style: Regardless of the format or platform, ensure your repurposed content maintains a consistent brand voice and visual identity.
4. Track the performance of your repurposed content: Monitor engagement and performance metrics for your repurposed content to understand its impact and identify areas for improvement.

Content repurposing is a powerful strategy for maximizing the value and reach of your existing content.

By adapting your content for various formats and platforms, you can connect with a wider audience, improve your SEO, and save time and resources. Embrace content repurposing as an essential part of your social media and content marketing strategy, ensuring your real estate business remains at the forefront of industry trends and best practices. As you continue to grow your online presence, be prepared to adapt and evolve your content repurposing strategies to meet the changing needs of your audience and the ever-evolving social media landscape.

CHAPTER 41:

STREAMLINING YOUR WORKFLOW

Efficiently managing your social media presence is crucial for real estate agents who want to make the most of their online marketing efforts. A streamlined workflow can help you save time, stay organized, and maintain consistency across all platforms. In this chapter, we will discuss various strategies and tools to help you streamline your social media workflow and optimize your productivity.

Plan & Organize Your Content

Planning and organizing your content in advance can help you maintain a consistent posting schedule and ensure your content aligns with your overall marketing strategy. Consider implementing the following practices:

- Develop a content calendar: Create a calendar outlining your content plan for each platform, including posting dates, themes, and topics. Update your calendar regularly to keep track of your content and stay organized.

- Use content themes or series: Implementing content themes or series can help you generate ideas and maintain consistency in your messaging.
- Schedule time for content creation: Set aside dedicated time in your schedule for content creation, ensuring you have ample time to research, write, and design high-quality content.

Utilize Automation Tools

Automation tools can save you time and help you maintain a consistent posting schedule. Explore these options:

1. Social media scheduling tools: Platforms like Hootsuite, Buffer, or Later allow you to schedule your posts in advance, so you can maintain a consistent presence across all platforms.
2. Content curation tools: Tools like Feedly or Pocket can help you discover and curate relevant content to share with your audience, saving you time on content research.
3. Analytics tools: Utilize analytics tools to track the performance of your content and gain insights into your audience's preferences and behavior. This can help you optimize your content strategy and improve your results.

Optimize Content Creation

Efficient content creation is essential for streamlining your workflow. Consider implementing these strategies:

1. Repurpose content: As discussed in the previous chapter, repurposing content can save you time and resources while maintaining a consistent message across platforms.
2. Use templates: Create templates for your social media posts, graphics, and other content to ensure a consistent visual identity and reduce the time spent on design.
3. Collaborate with others: Delegate content creation tasks to team members, or collaborate with other agents or businesses to share the workload.

Prioritize and Focus

Focusing on the most impactful tasks and platforms can help you optimize your productivity and ensure you're making the most of your social media efforts. Implement these strategies:

1. Identify your most effective platforms: Analyze your social media performance and focus your efforts on the platforms that drive the most engagement and results for your business.
2. Set realistic goals: Set achievable goals for your social media efforts, ensuring you can maintain a consistent presence without overextending your resources.
3. Prioritize high-impact tasks: Focus on the tasks that have the greatest impact on your social media presence and results, such as creating high-quality content or engaging with your audience.

Streamlining your workflow is essential for optimizing your social media efforts and making the most of your online presence.

By planning and organizing your content, utilizing automation tools, optimizing content creation, and focusing on high-impact tasks, you can save time, stay organized, and ensure your social media efforts are effective and efficient. As you continue to grow your real estate business, be prepared to adapt and refine your workflow to meet the changing needs of your audience and stay ahead of industry trends.

CHAPTER 42:

SOCIAL MEDIA ADVERTISING FOR REAL ESTATE AGENTS

Social media advertising has become an essential component of the digital marketing landscape for real estate agents. Paid ads on platforms like Facebook, Instagram, YouTube, and Pinterest can help you reach a larger audience, increase brand awareness, and generate leads more effectively. In this chapter, we will discuss the benefits of social media advertising and explore strategies for creating successful ad campaigns on various platforms.

Benefits of Social Media Advertising

- Targeted reach: Social media platforms offer advanced targeting options, allowing you to reach a highly specific audience based on demographics, interests, behaviors, and more.
- Cost-effective: Compared to traditional advertising methods, social media advertising is generally more cost-effective and offers a higher return on investment (ROI).

- Increased brand exposure: Social media ads can help you reach a larger audience, increasing your brand visibility and establishing your presence in the industry.
- Trackable results: Platforms like Facebook and Instagram offer in-depth analytics, allowing you to track the performance of your ads and optimize your campaigns based on data-driven insights.

Facebook Advertising

Facebook advertising is a popular choice for real estate agents due to its advanced targeting options and large user base. Consider the following strategies when creating your Facebook ad campaigns:

1. Choose the right objective: Facebook offers various campaign objectives, such as brand awareness, lead generation, and conversions. Select the objective that aligns with your overall marketing goals.
2. Utilize detailed targeting: Leverage Facebook's targeting options, such as demographics, interests, behaviors, and custom audiences, to reach your ideal audience.
3. Create engaging ad creatives: Design eye-catching visuals, write compelling ad copy, and consider utilizing video content to capture your audience's attention.
4. Test and optimize: Monitor your ad performance and test different targeting options, ad creatives, and placements to optimize your campaigns and improve your ROI.

Instagram Advertising

Instagram is a visually-driven platform that offers excellent opportunities for real estate agents to showcase their properties and engage with their target audience. Implement these strategies for your Instagram ad campaigns:

1. Utilize Stories and feed ads: Leverage both Instagram Stories and feed ads to reach a larger audience and increase engagement.
2. Showcase high-quality visuals: Use high-resolution images and videos to showcase your properties and create a strong visual identity for your brand.
3. Incorporate user-generated content: Include content from your clients, such as testimonials and property photos, to build trust and credibility with your audience.
4. Monitor and adjust: Keep an eye on your ad performance and make adjustments as needed to optimize your campaigns.

YouTube Advertising

YouTube offers a range of ad formats, including pre-roll, mid-roll, and display ads, which can help real estate agents increase brand visibility and generate leads. Consider these strategies for your YouTube ad campaigns:

1. Create engaging video content: Develop high-quality video content that showcases your properties, provides valuable information, and engages your audience.
2. Leverage targeting options: Use YouTube's targeting options, such as demographics, interests, and keywords, to reach your ideal audience.
3. Test different ad formats: Experiment with various ad formats and placements to determine what works best for your target audience and marketing goals.
4. Measure and optimize: Analyze your ad performance and make data-driven adjustments to improve your campaigns and maximize your ROI.

Pinterest Advertising

Pinterest is a visual platform that allows real estate agents to reach a highly engaged audience interested in home and design content. Implement these strategies for your Pinterest ad campaigns:

- Create visually-appealing Pins: Design high-quality, engaging Pins that showcase your properties and attract users' attention.
- Utilize keyword targeting Utilize keyword targeting: Leverage Pinterest's keyword targeting options to reach users who are actively searching for content related to your properties or services.
- Employ different ad formats: Experiment with various ad formats, such as promoted Pins and carousel ads, to increase engagement and drive results.

- Optimize for mobile: Ensure your Pins and ad creatives are optimized for mobile devices, as the majority of Pinterest users access the platform via their smartphones.
- Monitor and adjust: Keep track of your ad performance, and make data-driven adjustments to your targeting, creatives, and ad formats to continually improve your campaigns.

Best Practices for Social Media Advertising

Regardless of the platform you choose for your social media advertising efforts, consider implementing the following best practices to maximize your results:

1. Set clear objectives: Establish specific, measurable, achievable, relevant, and time-bound (SMART) goals for your ad campaigns to ensure they align with your overall marketing strategy.
2. Define your target audience: Clearly define your ideal audience and leverage the targeting options provided by each platform to reach them effectively.
3. Develop compelling ad creatives: Invest in high-quality visuals and engaging copy that capture your audience's attention and convey your unique value proposition.
4. Test and optimize: Continuously monitor your ad performance, and make data-driven adjustments to your campaigns to improve your results and ROI.
5. Allocate a budget: Determine a budget for your social media advertising efforts and allocate it strategically across platforms and campaigns.

Social media advertising offers a powerful way for real estate agents to reach a wider audience, generate leads, and grow their businesses. By understanding the benefits and best practices of advertising on platforms like Facebook, Instagram, YouTube, and Pinterest, you can develop effective campaigns that drive results and support your overall marketing strategy. Remember to monitor your ad performance, adjust your campaigns as needed, and stay up-to-date with industry trends and platform updates to maintain a competitive edge in the ever-evolving digital marketing landscape.

CHAPTER 43:

ADVERTISING BASICS

Before diving into the world of social media advertising for real estate agents, it's essential to understand the fundamentals of advertising. This chapter will cover the basic concepts and principles of advertising, as well as key strategies to ensure your ad campaigns are effective and yield the desired results.

The Purpose of Advertising

Advertising plays a crucial role in promoting your real estate services, generating leads, and increasing sales. The primary objectives of advertising are to:

- Create awareness: Introduce potential clients to your brand, services, and property listings.
- Generate interest: Captivate your target audience and pique their curiosity, encouraging them to learn more about your offerings.
- Encourage action: Drive potential clients to take specific actions,

such as contacting you for more information, booking a property viewing, or signing up for a newsletter.

- Build brand loyalty: Develop strong relationships with your clients and establish a positive brand reputation that encourages repeat business and referrals.

Advertising Principles

To create effective advertising campaigns, consider the following principles:

- AIDA Model: The AIDA (Attention, Interest, Desire, and Action) model is a widely-used framework that outlines the stages a consumer goes through when interacting with an advertisement. By understanding and addressing each stage, you can create ads that resonate with your audience and drive results.
- Targeting: Identifying and reaching your ideal audience is essential for successful advertising. Utilize the targeting options available on social media platforms to ensure your ads are seen by the right people.
- Unique Selling Proposition (USP): Your USP sets you apart from your competitors and highlights the unique benefits you offer. Clearly communicate your USP in your ad copy and visuals to attract your target audience.
- Consistency: Maintaining a consistent brand identity across your advertising efforts is crucial for building brand recognition and trust. Ensure your ad creatives align with your brand's voice, visual identity, and messaging.

- Testing and optimization: Continuously test different ad formats, targeting options, and creatives to determine what works best for your audience and goals. Use data-driven insights to optimize your campaigns and improve your ROI.

Ad Formats and Placements

Different social media platforms offer various ad formats and placements. Familiarize yourself with the options available on each platform and choose the ones that best suit your objectives and target audience. Some common ad formats include:

1. Image ads: Static images that showcase your properties, services, or brand.
2. Video ads: Engaging video content that captures your audience's attention and conveys your message more dynamically.
3. Carousel ads: A series of images or videos that users can swipe through, providing an interactive experience.
4. Story ads: Full-screen, immersive ads that appear between user-generated content on platforms like Instagram and Facebook.
5. Sponsored posts: Native ads that seamlessly blend into the user's feed on platforms like Facebook, Instagram, and Pinterest.

Ad Metrics and Performance Tracking

Monitor and analyze the performance of your ad campaigns to understand their effectiveness and make data-driven decisions. Key metrics to track include:

- Impressions: The number of times your ad was displayed.
- Clicks: The number of times users clicked on your ad.
- Click-through rate (CTR): The percentage of impressions that resulted in clicks.
- Conversions: The number of users who completed a desired action, such as contacting you, signing up for a newsletter, or booking a property viewing.
- Cost per click (CPC) or cost per thousand impressions (CPM): The amount you pay for each click or thousand ad impressions.
- Return on ad spend (ROAS): The revenue generated from your ad campaigns compared to the amount spent on advertising.
- Engagement rate: The percentage of users who interacted with your ad (e.g., likes, comments, shares) compared to the total number of impressions.
- Video view rate: The percentage of users who watched your video ad for a specific duration (e.g., 3 seconds, 10 seconds, or the entire video).

Creating a Comprehensive Advertising Plan

To maximize the impact of your advertising efforts, develop a comprehensive plan that outlines your objectives, target audience, budget, ad formats, and messaging. Consider the following steps:

- Set clear goals: Define your advertising objectives and ensure they align with your overall marketing strategy. Your goals should be specific, measurable, achievable, relevant, and time-bound (SMART).

- Identify your target audience: Determine the characteristics of your ideal clients, such as demographics, location, interests, and behaviors. Use this information to select the most appropriate targeting options on each social media platform.
- Allocate a budget: Establish a budget for your advertising efforts and allocate it strategically across platforms and campaigns. Consider factors like your objectives, target audience, and the costs associated with different ad formats and placements.
- Choose ad formats and placements: Select the most suitable ad formats and placements for your goals and target audience. Experiment with different options to determine what resonates best with your audience and yields the highest ROI.
- Develop compelling ad creatives: Invest in high-quality visuals and engaging ad copy that effectively communicate your unique value proposition and capture your audience's attention.
- Test and optimize: Monitor your ad performance and make data-driven adjustments to your campaigns, such as refining your targeting, updating your creatives, or trying new ad formats. Continuously optimize your campaigns to improve your results and maximize your ROI.
- Measure and analyze results: Regularly track and analyze your ad metrics to evaluate the success of your campaigns and gain insights into your audience's preferences and behaviors. Use this information to inform future advertising efforts and refine your overall marketing strategy.

Understanding advertising basics is crucial for real estate agents looking to leverage social media platforms to grow their businesses. By mastering fundamental advertising concepts, principles, and strategies, you can create more effective ad campaigns that resonate with your target audience and drive results. Remember to continuously monitor, test, and optimize your campaigns to maximize your ROI and stay ahead of the competition in the ever-evolving digital marketing landscape.

CHAPTER 44:

TARGETING OPTIONS

One of the key advantages of social media advertising for real estate agents is the ability to target your ideal audience with precision. Targeting options on various social media platforms allow you to reach the right people at the right time, increasing the effectiveness of your advertising efforts. This chapter will explore the different targeting options available and provide guidance on how to use them strategically to achieve your advertising objectives.

Demographic Targeting

Demographic targeting allows you to reach users based on characteristics such as age, gender, language, and education level. This type of targeting is essential for real estate agents looking to connect with potential clients who meet specific criteria. For example, you may want to target first-time homebuyers within a certain age range or focus on individuals who have recently moved to your area.

Geographic Targeting

Geographic targeting enables you to focus your advertising efforts on users located in specific areas, such as cities, regions, or countries. As a real estate agent, you can use geographic targeting to promote your services and listings to potential clients in your local market, as well as reach out-of-town buyers who may be interested in relocating.

Interest Targeting

Interest targeting allows you to target users based on their hobbies, interests, and behaviors. Social media platforms gather this information based on users' online activities, such as the pages they like, the content they engage with, and the websites they visit. As a real estate agent, you can use interest targeting to connect with potential clients who have shown an interest in real estate, home improvement, or interior design, for example.

Behavior Targeting

Behavior targeting focuses on users' past actions, such as their purchase history, device usage, and travel patterns. This information can help you reach potential clients who are more likely to be in the market for a new home or property. For instance, you can target users who have recently searched for homes online or visited real estate websites.

Custom Audiences

Custom audiences are a powerful targeting option that allows you to reach specific individuals based on your existing customer data. By uploading a list of email addresses or phone numbers, you can target users who have previously interacted with your business, such as past clients or newsletter subscribers. Custom audiences are particularly useful for retargeting campaigns, where you aim to re-engage users who have shown interest in your services or listings but have not yet taken action.

Lookalike Audiences

Lookalike audiences enable you to reach users who share similar characteristics with your existing customers or high-value prospects. Social media platforms use algorithms to identify users who are most likely to be interested in your offerings based on their similarities to your custom audience. Lookalike audiences can help you expand your reach and connect with potential clients who are more likely to convert.

Connection Targeting

Connection targeting focuses on users who have a relationship with your existing followers, such as friends of people who like your page or users who follow a specific account. By leveraging your existing audience's connections, you can tap into new networks and increase your brand visibility.

Strategies for Effective Targeting

To make the most of your social media advertising efforts, consider the following targeting strategies:

- Define your ideal client: Develop a clear understanding of your target audience, including their demographics, interests, behaviors, and geographic location. This information will help you make informed targeting decisions and create ads that resonate with your audience.
- Test and refine: Experiment with different targeting options to determine which ones generate the best results for your campaigns. Regularly review your ad performance and make data-driven adjustments to your targeting strategy.
- Combine targeting options: Use a combination of targeting options to narrow down your audience and reach the most relevant users. For example, you could target users in a specific geographic area who also have an interest in real estate and have recently engaged with similar content.
- Segment your campaigns: Create separate ad campaigns for different audience segments, allowing you to tailor your ad creative and messaging to each group. This approach can result in higher engagement rates and more effective ad spend.
- Monitor audience overlap: Be mindful of audience overlap between your campaigns, as targeting the same users across multiple campaigns can lead to ad fatigue and decreased performance. Use the audience overlap tools provided by social media platforms to identify and address any potential issues.

- Leverage retargeting: Use custom audiences and retargeting strategies to re-engage users who have previously interacted with your content or website. Retargeting campaigns can help remind potential clients of your services and encourage them to take action.
- Continuously update your targeting: As your business evolves and your target audience shifts, be sure to update your targeting strategies accordingly. Stay informed about new targeting options and features offered by social media platforms, and incorporate them into your advertising efforts as appropriate.

Effectively targeting your ideal audience is crucial to the success of your social media advertising campaigns. By understanding and utilizing the various targeting options available, you can maximize the impact of your ads and drive better results for your real estate business. Remember to continuously test, refine, and update your targeting strategies to ensure your campaigns remain relevant and effective in the ever-changing digital landscape.

CHAPTER 45:

AD FORMATS

Choosing the right ad format is essential for capturing your audience's attention and conveying your message effectively. Each social media platform offers a range of ad formats designed to cater to different objectives and content styles. This chapter will guide you through the various ad formats available on the major social media platforms and provide tips on how to use them effectively in your real estate advertising campaigns.

Facebook Ad Formats

- Image Ads: Image ads are a simple and effective way to showcase your property listings, promote your services, or share valuable content with your audience. Use high-quality images and concise, compelling copy to engage your target audience.
- Video Ads: Video ads allow you to tell a more immersive and engaging story about your properties, services, or brand.

Create short, attention-grabbing videos that showcase property tours, client testimonials, or neighborhood highlights.

- Carousel Ads: Carousel ads enable you to display multiple images or videos within a single ad unit, providing users with a richer and more interactive experience. Use carousel ads to showcase multiple property listings or highlight different aspects of a single property.
- Slideshow Ads: Slideshow ads combine multiple images, text, and sound to create a video-like ad experience. They are ideal for real estate agents who want to showcase a property's features or share a series of tips in a visually appealing format.
- Collection Ads: Collection ads allow you to feature a main video or image along with several smaller, clickable images. This format is perfect for showcasing a group of related properties or promoting a specific neighborhood or community.
- Lead Generation Ads: Lead generation ads are designed to capture user information, such as names and email addresses, directly within the ad unit. Use this format to encourage users to sign up for your newsletter, request a property valuation, or schedule a consultation.

Instagram Ad Formats

- Photo Ads: Similar to Facebook image ads, Instagram photo ads allow you to showcase your properties or services with a single, eye-catching image. Include a clear call-to-action and make sure your image stands out in the Instagram feed.
- Video Ads: Instagram video ads can be up to 60 seconds long, providing you with ample time to showcase your properties or tell a story about your brand. Keep your videos engaging and visually appealing to capture users' attention as they scroll through their feed.
- Carousel Ads: Instagram carousel ads work the same way as Facebook carousel ads, allowing you to feature multiple images or videos in a single ad unit. Use this format to highlight multiple property listings or provide a virtual tour of a property.
- Stories Ads: Instagram Stories ads appear between users' Stories content, providing a full-screen, immersive ad experience. Use attention-grabbing visuals and concise messaging to encourage users to swipe up and learn more about your offerings.
- IGTV Ads: IGTV ads allow you to create longer-form video content and monetize your IGTV channel. Use this format to share in-depth property tours, interviews, or educational content related to the real estate industry.

YouTube Ad Formats

- In-Stream Ads: In-stream ads play before, during, or after other videos on YouTube. These ads can be skippable or non-skippable and are an excellent way to reach a broad audience with your video content.
- Discovery Ads: Discovery ads appear alongside other videos on YouTube's search results, watch pages, and homepage. Use these ads to promote your video content and attract users who are actively searching for real estate-related topics.
- Bumper Ads: Bumper ads are short, non-skippable video ads that play before a user's chosen video. These ads are ideal for creating brand awareness and delivering a simple, memorable message to your target audience.
- Outstream Ads: Outstream ads are mobile-only video ads that play outside of YouTube, such as within apps or on partner websites. These ads provide additional reach and help you connect with users who may not be actively browsing YouTube.
- Masthead Ads: Masthead ads are high-impact ads that appear at the top of YouTube's homepage. This premium ad format is ideal for creating maximum visibility and reach for your real estate brand or a major campaign.

Pinterest Ad Formats

- Promoted Pins: Promoted Pins are regular Pins that you pay to promote, ensuring they reach a wider audience. Use high-quality images and concise descriptions to make your promoted Pins stand out and attract users interested in real estate.
- Video Pins: Video Pins allow you to share video content on Pinterest, providing an engaging and immersive experience for users. Create informative, visually appealing videos that showcase your properties or share valuable tips and insights.
- Carousel Pins: Carousel Pins enable you to feature up to five images within a single Pin. Use this format to showcase multiple property listings, highlight different aspects of a property, or share a series of related tips or insights.
- Promoted App Pins: Promoted App Pins allow you to promote your real estate app directly on Pinterest, driving users to download and engage with your app.

TikTok Ad Formats

- In-Feed Ads: In-feed ads appear within the user's For You feed on TikTok, seamlessly integrating with other content. These short, engaging video ads are perfect for capturing users' attention and showcasing your real estate offerings.
- Branded Hashtag Challenges: Branded hashtag challenges encourage users to create and share content using your custom hashtag, driving user-generated content and engagement around your brand or campaign.
- Branded Effects: Branded effects are custom filters, stickers, or animations that users can apply to their TikTok videos. Create a branded effect related to your real estate business to encourage users to engage with your brand and share content with their followers.

Selecting the right ad format for your real estate campaigns is crucial to maximizing engagement and driving results. Familiarize yourself with the various formats available on each social media platform and choose the ones that best align with your advertising objectives, target audience, and content style. Continuously test and refine your ad creative to ensure your campaigns are as effective as possible and consistently deliver value to your audience.

CHAPTER 46:

BUDGETING AND CREATING HIGH-CONVERTING ADS

A crucial aspect of any successful social media advertising campaign is allocating a budget and creating high-converting ads that resonate with your target audience. In this chapter, we'll discuss strategies for setting an appropriate budget and tips for crafting compelling ads that drive results.

Budgeting for Social Media Advertising

Setting a budget for your advertising campaigns is an essential step in ensuring that your marketing efforts are financially sustainable and generate a positive return on investment (ROI). Here are some factors to consider when budgeting for social media advertising:

- Marketing goals: Determine the primary objectives of your advertising campaigns. Are you trying to build brand awareness, generate leads, or drive property sales? Your marketing goals will influence your budget allocation.

- Target audience: Identify your target audience and their behavior on different social media platforms. Some platforms may require a higher budget due to increased competition or higher cost-per-click (CPC) rates.
- Platform-specific costs: Each social media platform has its own pricing structure for advertising. Research the costs associated with your chosen platforms and factor them into your budget.
- Testing and optimization: Allocate a portion of your budget for testing various ad formats, creatives, and targeting options. This will enable you to optimize your campaigns for better performance over time.
- Monitoring and adjusting: Regularly track the performance of your ads and adjust your budget as needed. This will ensure that you're allocating your resources effectively and maximizing your ROI.

Creating High-Converting Ads

High-converting ads are essential for driving results and achieving your marketing goals. Here are some tips for creating ads that resonate with your target audience and encourage them to take action:

- Use high-quality visuals: High-quality images and videos are essential for capturing users' attention and showcasing your properties in the best light. Invest in professional photography and videography to create visually appealing content.

- Craft compelling headlines: Your ad's headline should be attention-grabbing and clearly communicate the value proposition of your offering. Use strong action verbs and descriptive language to entice users to click on your ad.
- Write persuasive ad copy: Your ad copy should be concise, informative, and persuasive. Clearly communicate the benefits of your properties or services and include a clear call-to-action (CTA) that encourages users to take the desired action.
- Utilize social proof: Incorporate testimonials, ratings, or success stories into your ads to build trust with your audience and demonstrate the value of your real estate services.
- Optimize for mobile: Ensure that your ads are mobile-friendly and display properly on various devices. With the majority of social media users accessing platforms via mobile devices, it's essential to provide a seamless user experience.
- Test and iterate: Regularly test different ad creatives, headlines, and copy to determine what resonates best with your audience. Use the insights gathered from your tests to optimize your ads and improve their performance.

Budgeting and creating high-converting ads are essential components of any successful social media advertising campaign. By setting a realistic budget, considering platform-specific costs, and crafting compelling ads that resonate with your target audience, you can maximize the effectiveness of your campaigns and achieve your marketing goals.

CHAPTER 47:

SOCIAL MEDIA ANALYTICS AND TRACKING SUCCESS

Social media analytics play a critical role in measuring the success of your real estate marketing efforts. By closely monitoring your campaign performance, you can make data-driven decisions, optimize your strategies, and ensure you're achieving the best possible results. This chapter will guide you through the key aspects of social media analytics and how to track the success of your real estate campaigns.

Understanding Social Media Metrics

To effectively track the success of your campaigns, it's essential to understand the different social media metrics and what they signify. Here are some important metrics to consider:

- Reach: The number of unique users who have seen your content.
- Impressions: The total number of times your content has been displayed.
- Engagement: The number of interactions your content receives, such as likes, comments, shares, and clicks.

- Click-through rate (CTR): The percentage of users who click on your ad or content after seeing it.
- Conversion rate: The percentage of users who complete a desired action, such as submitting a contact form or scheduling a property viewing.

Selecting Key Performance Indicators (KPIs)

Key performance indicators (KPIs) are specific metrics that you'll use to measure the success of your campaigns. To choose the right KPIs for your real estate marketing efforts, consider your primary objectives. For instance, if your main goal is to generate leads, your KPIs may include the number of new leads, the cost per lead, and the conversion rate.

Using Analytics Tools

Leverage the built-in analytics tools provided by each social media platform to track your campaign performance. These tools offer valuable insights into your audience demographics, user behavior, and the effectiveness of your content. Some popular social media analytics tools include:

1. Facebook Insights
2. Instagram Insights
3. YouTube Analytics
4. Pinterest Analytics
5. Twitter Analytics

Additionally, you may consider using third-party analytics tools like Hootsuite, Sprout Social, or Google Analytics for more in-depth data analysis and reporting.

Setting Benchmarks and Goals

Establish benchmarks and set realistic goals for your social media campaigns. Use industry averages and your past performance data as a starting point to set achievable targets. Continuously monitor your progress and adjust your goals as needed to ensure you're on track to meet your objectives.

A/B Testing and Optimization

A/B testing is a crucial component of tracking success and optimizing your social media campaigns. By testing different variables, such as ad creatives, headlines, and targeting options, you can identify which elements perform best and refine your strategies accordingly.

Reporting and Evaluation

Create regular reports to analyze your social media performance, track your progress toward your goals, and identify areas for improvement. Share these reports with your team and use the insights to make data-driven decisions that drive your real estate business forward.

Social media analytics and tracking success are essential aspects of any effective real estate marketing campaign. By understanding key metrics, selecting the right KPIs, and utilizing analytics tools, you can make informed decisions and optimize your strategies for the best possible results.

CHAPTER 48:

KEY METRICS TO TRACK

To effectively measure the success of your social media marketing efforts, it's crucial to track the right key performance indicators (KPIs). By focusing on the most relevant metrics, you can gain valuable insights into your campaign performance, identify areas for improvement, and optimize your strategies. In this chapter, we'll explore the key metrics real estate agents should track to ensure their social media campaigns are successful.

Reach and Impressions

Reach and impressions are essential metrics to gauge your brand's visibility on social media platforms. Reach measures the total number of unique users who have seen your content, while impressions represent the total number of times your content has been displayed to users. Tracking these metrics helps you understand the overall exposure of your content and identify the potential audience size for your campaigns.

Engagement Metrics

Engagement metrics provide insights into how users interact with your content. Key engagement metrics include:

1. Likes: The number of users who liked your content.
2. Comments: The total number of comments your content received.
3. Shares: The number of times your content was shared by users.
4. Clicks: The total number of clicks on your content, such as links, images, or videos.

By tracking these metrics, you can assess the effectiveness of your content, identify the types of content that resonate with your audience, and optimize your content strategy accordingly.

Follower Growth

Monitoring your follower growth is crucial to understanding how your online presence is expanding over time. A steady increase in followers indicates that your content and branding resonate with your target audience. Pay attention to sudden spikes or drops in follower count, as these can signal potential issues or opportunities in your social media strategy.

Click-Through Rate (CTR)

CTR measures the percentage of users who click on your content or ads after seeing them. This metric is particularly important for assessing the effectiveness of your paid advertising campaigns.

A higher CTR indicates that your ads are relevant and engaging to your target audience. By monitoring your CTR, you can identify which ads perform best and optimize your ad creatives and targeting accordingly.

Conversion Rate

Conversion rate is a critical metric for determining the effectiveness of your social media campaigns in driving desired actions, such as filling out a contact form, signing up for a newsletter, or scheduling a property viewing. By tracking your conversion rate, you can assess the overall success of your campaigns and identify areas for improvement.

Cost Per Action (CPA)

CPA measures the average cost of acquiring a lead or customer through your social media campaigns. This metric is essential for understanding the return on investment (ROI) of your marketing efforts. To optimize your CPA, focus on improving your targeting, ad creatives, and landing pages.

Social Media ROI

ROI is the ultimate metric for evaluating the success of your social media marketing efforts. By calculating your social media ROI, you can determine the profitability of your campaigns and make data-driven decisions about your marketing budget allocation. To calculate ROI, compare the revenue generated by your campaigns to the total cost of your social media marketing efforts.

Tracking the right key metrics is essential for measuring the success of your social media campaigns and optimizing your marketing strategies. By focusing on reach, impressions, engagement, follower growth, CTR, conversion rate, CPA, and ROI, you can gain valuable insights into your campaign performance, identify areas for improvement, and ensure your social media efforts are driving tangible results for your real estate business.

CHAPTER 49:

SOCIAL MEDIA ANALYTICS TOOLS

Using the right social media analytics tools is crucial for tracking, analyzing, and optimizing your social media marketing campaigns. These tools can help you gain valuable insights into your target audience, monitor key performance indicators, and improve your overall social media strategy. In this chapter, we'll explore some of the most popular and powerful social media analytics tools that real estate agents can use to enhance their social media marketing efforts.

Native Social Media Analytics Tools

Most social media platforms offer built-in analytics tools that provide insights into your account's performance. These native tools can help you understand your audience demographics, content performance, and engagement metrics.

1. Facebook Insights: Access a wide range of analytics for your Facebook Page, including reach, impressions, engagement, follower growth, and more.
2. Instagram Insights: Monitor your Instagram profile's performance, including follower demographics, content engagement, and reach.
3. YouTube Analytics: Analyze your YouTube channel's performance, including video views, watch time, audience retention, and more.
4. Pinterest Analytics: Track your Pinterest account's performance, including impressions, saves, clicks, and audience demographics.
5. TikTok Analytics: Gain insights into your TikTok account's performance, including profile views, follower growth, and content engagement.

Third-Party Analytics Tools

In addition to the native analytics tools provided by social media platforms, there are many third-party tools available that offer advanced analytics features and functionality.

- Hootsuite: A comprehensive social media management platform that includes powerful analytics features, allowing you to track your performance across multiple social media platforms in one place.
- Sprout Social: A social media management tool with in-depth analytics capabilities, offering customizable reports and insights to help optimize your social media strategy.

- SocialBakers: A social media analytics platform that provides a comprehensive suite of tools for tracking, analyzing, and optimizing your social media performance.
- Iconosquare: A specialized analytics tool for Instagram and Facebook, offering insights into content performance, audience growth, and engagement.
- Google Analytics: Although not specifically a social media analytics tool, Google Analytics can be used to track website traffic and conversions from your social media campaigns.

Social Media Listening Tools

Social media listening tools can help you monitor online conversations about your brand, industry, and competitors. These tools can provide valuable insights into customer sentiment, identify potential leads, and help you stay ahead of industry trends.

1. Brand24: A social media listening tool that helps you track online conversations about your brand and industry, monitor sentiment, and identify potential leads.
2. Mention: A comprehensive social media listening platform that enables you to monitor mentions of your brand, competitors, and industry across various social media platforms and websites.
3. Awario: A social media listening tool that offers real-time monitoring of brand mentions, sentiment analysis, and competitor tracking.

Utilizing the right social media analytics tools is crucial for optimizing your social media marketing efforts. By leveraging native analytics tools and third-party solutions, you can gain valuable insights into your campaign performance, track key metrics, and refine your social media strategy. Additionally, social media listening tools can help you monitor online conversations and stay ahead of industry trends. By investing in the right analytics tools, real estate agents can ensure their social media efforts are driving tangible results and continuously improving their marketing strategies.

CHAPTER 50:

INTERPRETING DATA AND OPTIMIZING YOUR STRATEGY

Data-driven decision making is essential for optimizing your social media strategy and ensuring the best possible results from your marketing efforts. Interpreting data from various analytics tools can help you identify trends, discover what works, and make informed decisions about your content, targeting, and overall approach. In this chapter, we will discuss how real estate agents can interpret data from their social media analytics and use these insights to optimize their strategy.

Identifying Patterns and Trends

The first step in interpreting your social media data is to identify patterns and trends. Look for recurring themes in your content performance, audience demographics, and engagement metrics. These patterns can reveal valuable insights into what resonates with your audience and what types of content drive the best results.

For example, you may discover that video content generates more engagement than static images or that certain topics consistently outperform others.

Benchmarking Performance

To effectively measure your social media success, it's crucial to establish benchmarks for your key performance indicators (KPIs). Compare your performance against these benchmarks to determine whether your strategy is on track or needs adjustment. Consider industry averages and competitor data to provide context and ensure your benchmarks are realistic and achievable.

A/B Testing

A/B testing, or split testing, is a method of comparing two variations of a single variable to determine which performs better. This can be applied to various aspects of your social media strategy, such as ad creatives, targeting options, and content formats. Use the insights gained from A/B testing to refine and optimize your strategy, ensuring you are using the most effective tactics for your target audience and objectives.

Adjusting Your Strategy

Once you have identified trends, established benchmarks, and conducted A/B tests, use these insights to adjust and optimize your social media strategy.

This may involve experimenting with new content formats, targeting different audience segments, or adjusting your posting schedule. Continuously monitoring your performance and making data-driven adjustments will help you maximize your social media marketing efforts and achieve your desired results.

Maintaining a Growth Mindset

In the rapidly evolving world of social media, it's essential to maintain a growth mindset and be open to change. Embrace new technologies, platforms, and trends as they emerge and use your data-driven insights to adapt your strategy accordingly. By staying agile and responsive, you can ensure your social media efforts remain relevant and effective in the ever-changing digital landscape.

Interpreting data from your social media analytics and using these insights to optimize your strategy is crucial for achieving success as a real estate agent in today's competitive market. By identifying trends, benchmarking performance, conducting A/B tests, and adjusting your approach based on data-driven insights, you can continuously improve your social media marketing efforts and drive better results for your business. Embrace a growth mindset and be open to change, ensuring your social media strategy remains relevant and effective in an ever-evolving digital landscape.

CHAPTER 51:

BUILDING AND MANAGING YOUR ONLINE REPUTATION

In the digital age, your online reputation can make or break your real estate business. With potential clients increasingly turning to the internet to research agents, it's essential to build and maintain a positive online presence. This chapter will cover strategies for building and managing your online reputation, ensuring you create a strong and trustworthy brand image.

Importance of Online Reputation

Your online reputation is the perception that people have of your real estate business based on information available on the internet. A strong online reputation can lead to increased trust, more referrals, and a higher likelihood of clients choosing to work with you. Conversely, a poor online reputation can result in lost opportunities and a negative impact on your business.

Building Your Online Reputation

To build a positive online reputation, focus on the following key areas:

a. Consistent Branding: Ensure your branding is consistent across all online platforms, from your website to your social media profiles. This helps create a cohesive brand image and makes it easier for potential clients to recognize and remember your business.

b. Quality Content: Share valuable and informative content that showcases your expertise and knowledge of the real estate market. This helps position you as a trusted authority in your field and attracts potential clients.

c. Online Reviews: Encourage satisfied clients to leave reviews on platforms like Google, Facebook, and Yelp. Positive reviews can significantly impact your online reputation, as potential clients often rely on these testimonials when selecting a real estate agent.

d. Responsive Communication: Respond promptly to inquiries and messages on social media and other online platforms. This demonstrates your commitment to providing excellent customer service and helps build trust with potential clients.

Monitoring Your Online Reputation

Regularly monitor your online reputation by doing the following:

a. Set up Google Alerts: Set up alerts for your name and your real estate business to receive notifications when new content is published about you online.

b. Check Review Sites: Regularly check review sites and respond to both positive and negative feedback in a professional and courteous manner.

c. Analyze Social Media Mentions: Use social media monitoring tools to track mentions of your brand and address any concerns or questions in a timely fashion.

Managing Negative Feedback

Negative feedback is inevitable, but how you handle it can make a significant difference in your online reputation. When addressing negative feedback:

a. Respond promptly and professionally: Acknowledge the issue and apologize if necessary. Offer a solution or explain how you will work to resolve the problem.

b. Take the conversation offline: If possible, invite the person to contact you directly to discuss the matter further. This can help prevent an online dispute and shows your commitment to addressing the issue.

c. Learn from the feedback: Use negative feedback as an opportunity to identify areas where you can improve your service and make changes accordingly.

Building and managing your online reputation is crucial for success in the real estate industry. By focusing on consistent branding, quality content, online reviews, and responsive communication, you can establish a positive online presence that attracts and retains clients.

Regularly monitor your reputation and address negative feedback in a professional and constructive manner to maintain a strong and trustworthy brand image.

CHAPTER 52:

MONITORING REVIEWS

Monitoring reviews is a vital aspect of managing your online reputation as a real estate agent. Reviews can significantly influence potential clients' decisions when choosing an agent. In this chapter, we will discuss strategies and tools to help you monitor reviews effectively, respond to them, and use the feedback to improve your business.

Importance of Reviews

Online reviews play a critical role in shaping your online reputation. Positive reviews can boost your credibility and trustworthiness, leading to more clients and referrals. Negative reviews, on the other hand, can damage your reputation and deter potential clients. Monitoring and addressing reviews can help you maintain a positive online presence and address any concerns before they escalate.

Review Monitoring Strategies

To effectively monitor reviews, consider implementing the following strategies:

a. Identify Relevant Review Platforms: Determine the most relevant platforms where your clients are likely to leave reviews, such as Google, Facebook, Yelp, Zillow, and Realtor.com. Focus your monitoring efforts on these platforms.

b. Schedule Regular Check-ins: Set aside time in your weekly schedule to check for new reviews on each platform. This ensures that you stay up-to-date with client feedback and can respond promptly.

c. Use Monitoring Tools: Utilize tools and software that can help you monitor reviews more efficiently. Many review platforms offer built-in monitoring features, or you can use third-party tools like ReviewTrackers or Yext to consolidate and manage reviews across multiple platforms.

Responding to Reviews

Responding to both positive and negative reviews is essential for maintaining a positive online reputation:

a. Respond to Positive Reviews: Thank your clients for their kind words and express gratitude for their feedback. Responding to positive reviews shows appreciation and reinforces the positive experience.

b. Address Negative Reviews: Respond to negative reviews professionally and empathetically. Apologize if necessary, and offer a solution or explain how you will work to resolve the issue. If possible, take the conversation offline to discuss the matter further.

c. Be Timely: Respond to reviews as quickly as possible. A prompt response shows your commitment to excellent customer service and can help mitigate any potential damage from negative feedback.

Learning from Reviews

Reviews can be a valuable source of feedback, helping you identify areas for improvement in your business. Analyze reviews to spot trends or recurring issues and take action to address them. By addressing concerns proactively, you can enhance your services, leading to increased client satisfaction and more positive reviews.

Encouraging More Reviews

A higher number of positive reviews can help boost your online reputation. Encourage clients to leave reviews by:
a. Requesting Reviews: Politely ask satisfied clients to leave a review on the platform of their choice. Many clients are happy to share their positive experiences when asked.
b. Make It Easy: Provide clients with direct links to your review profiles, making it convenient for them to leave feedback.
c. Incentivize Reviews: Offer incentives, like discounts or small gifts, as a token of appreciation for clients who leave reviews. However, ensure that you are adhering to the guidelines of each review platform.

Monitoring and managing reviews is essential for maintaining a positive online reputation in the real estate industry. Implement effective monitoring strategies, respond to reviews professionally, and use client feedback to improve your services. By staying on top of reviews, you can strengthen your online presence, attract more clients, and ultimately, grow your business.

CHAPTER 53:

HANDLING NEGATIVE FEEDBACK

Negative feedback is an inevitable part of any business, and the real estate industry is no exception. Dealing with negative feedback effectively can help protect your online reputation and turn unhappy clients into satisfied ones. This chapter will provide strategies and best practices for handling negative feedback on social media and other online platforms.

The Importance of Addressing Negative Feedback

Ignoring negative feedback can have serious consequences for your real estate business. Addressing negative feedback is essential for maintaining a positive online reputation, demonstrating your commitment to customer satisfaction, and learning valuable lessons to improve your business.

Assessing the Feedback

Before responding to negative feedback, it's important to assess the situation:

a. Evaluate the Validity: Determine if the feedback is legitimate or simply the result of a misunderstanding. This will help you craft an appropriate response.

b. Identify Recurring Issues: Keep track of negative feedback to identify patterns or recurring issues. Addressing these concerns can lead to significant improvements in your services and client satisfaction.

Responding to Negative Feedback

Follow these steps when responding to negative feedback:

a. Stay Calm and Professional: Keep your emotions in check and maintain a professional tone when addressing negative feedback.

b. Respond in a Timely Manner: Responding quickly to negative feedback shows that you take your clients' concerns seriously and are committed to addressing their issues.

c. Apologize and Empathize: Offer a sincere apology if appropriate, and show empathy for the client's experience.

d. Offer a Solution: Propose a solution to the issue or explain the steps you will take to resolve the problem. This demonstrates your commitment to making things right.

e. Take the Conversation Offline: If necessary, invite the client to discuss the matter privately through email or phone. This can help you resolve the issue more effectively and avoid a public dispute.

Learning from Negative Feedback

Use negative feedback as an opportunity to improve your real estate business:

a. Address the Root Cause: Identify the root cause of the issue and implement changes to prevent similar problems in the future.

b. Train Your Team: Share negative feedback with your team and use it as a learning opportunity. This will help them understand the importance of addressing client concerns and improve their skills in handling difficult situations.

Turning Negative Feedback into a Positive Outcome

By addressing negative feedback effectively, you can turn a potentially damaging situation into a positive outcome:

a. Showcase Your Commitment to Customer Service: Responding to negative feedback demonstrates your dedication to providing excellent customer service and resolving client issues.

b. Foster Client Loyalty: Clients who have their concerns addressed effectively are more likely to remain loyal to your business and recommend you to others.

c. Strengthen Your Online Reputation: Addressing negative feedback can help mitigate its impact on your online reputation and potentially turn a dissatisfied client into a satisfied one.

Handling negative feedback is a crucial aspect of managing your online reputation as a real estate agent. By addressing feedback professionally and empathetically, offering solutions, and learning from your clients' concerns, you can turn negative situations into opportunities for growth and positive outcomes for your business.

CHAPTER 54:

ENCOURAGING POSITIVE REVIEWS

Positive reviews play a vital role in enhancing your online reputation and attracting potential clients. By actively encouraging clients to share their positive experiences, you can leverage the power of social proof to grow your real estate business. This chapter will provide strategies and best practices for encouraging positive reviews from your clients.

The Importance of Positive Reviews

Positive reviews can significantly impact your real estate business by:

a. Building Trust: Potential clients are more likely to trust a real estate agent with a strong track record of positive reviews.
b. Improving Online Visibility: Positive reviews can boost your search engine rankings and increase your visibility on review platforms and social media sites.

c. Generating Referrals: Satisfied clients are more likely to recommend your services to their friends, family, and colleagues.

Providing Exceptional Service

The foundation of earning positive reviews is providing exceptional service. Focus on exceeding your clients' expectations at every stage of the real estate process to create memorable experiences that inspire them to leave positive feedback.

Asking for Reviews

Don't be afraid to ask clients for reviews. Follow these best practices when requesting feedback:

a. Choose the Right Timing: The best time to ask for a review is when the client is most satisfied with your service, such as after a successful closing.
b. Make It Personal: Personalize your request by mentioning specific details of your interaction with the client. This demonstrates your genuine interest in their feedback.
c. Offer Multiple Platforms: Provide clients with a choice of review platforms, such as Google, Facebook, or Yelp, to make it easy for them to leave a review.

Simplifying the Review Process

Make it as simple as possible for clients to leave a review:
a. Provide Clear Instructions: Explain the review process step by step, and include links to the review platforms in your email or message.
b. Use Review Generation Tools: Consider using review generation tools, such as GatherUp or Podium, to automate the review request process and make it easier for clients to provide feedback.

Showcasing Positive Reviews

Promote your positive reviews to showcase your expertise and commitment to client satisfaction:
a. Share Reviews on Social Media: Share positive reviews on your social media channels to increase your credibility and reach.
b. Feature Reviews on Your Website: Add a testimonials section to your website to display positive reviews from satisfied clients.
c. Include Reviews in Marketing Materials: Incorporate client testimonials into your marketing materials, such as email campaigns, brochures, and presentations.

Responding to Positive Reviews

Thank clients for their positive feedback and demonstrate your appreciation for their business:
a. Acknowledge Their Praise: Show your gratitude by acknowledging the specific aspects of your service they praised.

b. Highlight Your Core Values: Reinforce your commitment to exceptional service by mentioning your core values or mission statement.

c. Encourage Referrals: Express your willingness to assist the client's friends or family members with their real estate needs and encourage them to refer your services.

Positive reviews are essential for establishing trust, improving online visibility, and generating referrals for your real estate business. By providing exceptional service, simplifying the review process, and showcasing positive feedback, you can encourage satisfied clients to share their experiences and help you grow your business.

CHAPTER 55:

THE FUTURE OF SOCIAL MEDIA IN REAL ESTATE

As technology and social media platforms continue to evolve, real estate agents must stay ahead of the curve to remain competitive in the industry. This chapter will explore the potential future trends of social media in real estate, highlighting how agents can prepare and adapt to the changing landscape.

Emerging Social Media Platforms

While Facebook, Instagram, TikTok, YouTube, and Pinterest have dominated the real estate social media landscape, emerging platforms are likely to provide new opportunities for agents to connect with their audience:

a. Virtual Reality Platforms: Platforms such as Spatial and VRChat may enable virtual property tours and immersive, interactive experiences for clients.

b. Audio-Based Platforms: With the rise of audio-focused platforms like Clubhouse, real estate professionals can participate in or host discussions, share expertise, and network with potential clients.

c. Niche Social Networks: As niche social networks gain popularity, real estate agents should explore platforms tailored to specific interests or demographics, such as Nextdoor, which connects neighbors within a specific community.

Advanced Technologies

Technological advancements are poised to shape the future of social media in real estate:

a. Artificial Intelligence (AI): AI-powered chatbots and content creation tools can streamline communication, customer service, and social media management for real estate agents.

b. Augmented Reality (AR): AR technology, such as Snapchat's AR filters or Instagram's AR effects, can provide interactive experiences, allowing clients to visualize property improvements or virtually "stage" homes.

c. Big Data and Analytics: Advanced data analysis tools will enable real estate agents to better understand their audience, predict trends, and create targeted marketing campaigns.

Personalization and Hyper-Targeting

As consumers increasingly expect personalized experiences, real estate agents must adapt their social media strategies to deliver relevant, tailored content:

a. Customized Content: Use data-driven insights to create content that speaks to the specific needs, preferences, and pain points of your target audience.

b. Location-Based Marketing: Leverage location data to target potential clients in specific geographic areas with tailored messaging and offers.

c. Behavioral Targeting: Analyze user behavior on social media platforms to serve highly relevant content and ads based on their interests and online activity.

Ethical Considerations and Privacy Regulations

As concerns about data privacy and ethical use of technology grow, real estate agents must stay informed about evolving regulations and best practices:

a. Data Privacy: Familiarize yourself with privacy regulations, such as GDPR and CCPA, and ensure your social media practices comply with these rules.

b. Transparency and Authenticity: Build trust with your audience by being transparent about your data collection and usage practices and maintaining an authentic, genuine presence on social media.

c. Responsible Use of Technology: Be mindful of potential ethical concerns when implementing new technologies, such as AI or facial recognition, and prioritize the best interests of your clients.

The future of social media in real estate will be shaped by emerging platforms, advanced technologies, personalization, and ethical considerations.

Staying informed about these trends and adapting your social media strategy accordingly will help you remain competitive and successfully navigate the ever-evolving digital landscape.

CHAPTER 56:

EMERGING TRENDS

As the real estate industry continues to evolve, it is essential for agents to stay informed about emerging trends to stay competitive and provide the best possible service to their clients. This chapter will discuss some of the latest trends in real estate and social media and explore how they may impact your business.

Remote Work and the Demand for Home Offices

The shift towards remote work has significantly impacted the real estate industry. As more people work from home, the demand for dedicated home office spaces has increased. Real estate agents should consider highlighting home office features on their social media channels and showcasing properties that cater to this growing need.

Sustainable and Eco-Friendly Homes

As concerns about climate change and the environment grow, many homebuyers are seeking eco-friendly and sustainable housing options. Real estate agents can capitalize on this trend by sharing information about green building materials, energy-efficient technologies, and environmentally friendly home design on their social media platforms.

The Rise of Co-Living Spaces

Co-living spaces, where residents share common areas and amenities, are becoming increasingly popular, particularly in urban areas with high housing costs. Real estate agents should consider showcasing co-living properties on their social media channels and highlighting the benefits of this housing trend, such as affordability and community-building.

Smart Home Technologies

Smart home technologies, such as automation systems, security features, and energy-efficient appliances, are becoming more prevalent in new homes. Real estate agents can leverage this trend by showcasing smart home features on their social media platforms and educating potential buyers about the benefits of these technologies.

Virtual and Augmented Reality in Real Estate

As mentioned in previous chapters, virtual and augmented reality technologies are revolutionizing the real estate industry. From virtual property tours to AR-enhanced property listings, these technologies enable agents to provide immersive, interactive experiences for clients. Stay informed about the latest advancements in VR and AR and incorporate them into your social media strategy to stay ahead of the competition.

The Importance of Community and Neighborhood

More than ever, homebuyers are looking for properties that offer a strong sense of community and connection to the neighborhood. Real estate agents can tap into this trend by sharing information about local events, businesses, and community initiatives on their social media channels, showcasing the unique aspects of the neighborhoods they serve.

The Growing Popularity of Short-Term Rentals

The short-term rental market, driven by platforms like Airbnb and VRBO, has experienced significant growth in recent years. Real estate agents should consider showcasing properties with short-term rental potential on their social media channels and providing information about local regulations and potential income opportunities for buyers.

Staying informed about emerging trends in real estate and social media is crucial for agents looking to stay competitive and provide the best possible service to their clients. By understanding and adapting to these trends, you can position yourself as a forward-thinking, knowledgeable expert in your field and continue to grow your business in an ever-changing industry.

CHAPTER 57:

NEW PLATFORMS AND OPPORTUNITIES

As technology evolves and new social media platforms emerge, real estate agents must stay abreast of the latest developments to capitalize on new opportunities for marketing and networking. This chapter will discuss some of the emerging social media platforms and other digital channels that real estate agents should consider exploring to stay ahead of the competition and reach new audiences.

Clubhouse and Audio-Only Platforms

Clubhouse, an audio-only social media platform, has gained significant popularity for its real-time conversations and networking opportunities. Real estate agents can leverage Clubhouse by hosting or participating in discussions about the real estate industry, sharing insights, and connecting with potential clients and industry peers. Keep an eye on similar audio-only platforms as they emerge, as they could offer unique opportunities for engagement and networking.

Virtual Reality (VR) Platforms

As mentioned in previous chapters, virtual reality is playing an increasingly significant role in the real estate industry. Platforms like Spatial and AltspaceVR provide virtual spaces where users can meet, collaborate, and engage in immersive experiences. Real estate agents can use these platforms to host virtual open houses, offer property tours, and engage with clients in innovative ways.

Blockchain and Decentralized Social Networks

Blockchain technology has the potential to revolutionize the way we interact on social media, with decentralized platforms offering increased privacy, security, and control over personal data. As decentralized social networks like Mastodon and Minds gain traction, real estate agents should consider establishing a presence on these platforms to connect with potential clients who value privacy and digital autonomy.

Niche Social Media Platforms

While mainstream platforms like Facebook and Instagram remain important, niche social media platforms catering to specific interests and communities offer unique opportunities for real estate agents to connect with potential clients. For example, Houzz, a platform dedicated to home design and renovation, could be an ideal place for agents to showcase their listings' unique features and connect with homebuyers interested in design.

Influencer Partnerships and Collaborations

Influencer marketing continues to grow in popularity, with brands leveraging the reach and credibility of social media influencers to promote their products and services. Real estate agents can collaborate with influencers in the home and design space, local influencers, or even micro-influencers within their target market to increase their brand visibility and reach new audiences.

Live Streaming Platforms

Live streaming platforms like Twitch, Facebook Live, and YouTube Live offer real-time interaction opportunities, allowing real estate agents to engage with their audience in a more personal and authentic way. Consider hosting live property tours, Q&A sessions, or even informal chats to connect with potential clients and showcase your expertise.

Short-Form Video Platforms

Short-form video platforms like TikTok have become wildly popular, offering a unique way to engage with audiences through bite-sized, easily consumable content. Keep an eye on emerging short-form video platforms and consider experimenting with different content formats to see what resonates with your target audience.

As new platforms and digital channels continue to emerge, real estate agents must adapt and evolve their social media strategies to stay ahead of the competition and reach new audiences. By exploring these emerging platforms and opportunities, you can create a diverse and robust online presence that positions you as a forward-thinking and innovative leader in the real estate industry.

CHAPTER 58:

LIVE STREAMING AND VIRTUAL REALITY

The rapid advancements in technology have significantly impacted the way we communicate and consume content. Live streaming and virtual reality (VR) are two such technological innovations that have gained popularity in recent years. Both offer unique opportunities for real estate agents to engage with their audience, showcase properties, and deliver immersive experiences. This chapter will delve into the potential of live streaming and virtual reality for real estate agents and offer tips and strategies for incorporating these technologies into your marketing efforts.

Live Streaming for Real Estate

Live streaming provides real-time interaction opportunities, allowing real estate agents to engage with their audience in a more personal and authentic way. Some popular live streaming platforms include Facebook Live, YouTube Live, Instagram Live, and Twitch.

Hosting Virtual Open Houses

One practical application of live streaming for real estate agents is hosting virtual open houses. By broadcasting live from a property, you can give potential buyers an exclusive, real-time tour while addressing their questions and concerns in the comments section.

Q&A Sessions

Live streaming Q&A sessions allow real estate agents to share their expertise, offer valuable insights, and answer questions from potential clients. These interactive sessions can help establish you as an industry expert and build trust with your audience.

Behind-the-Scenes Content

Sharing behind-the-scenes content, such as property walkthroughs, neighborhood tours, or a day in the life of a real estate agent, can offer a unique perspective and humanize your brand. This can help forge a deeper connection with your audience and give them an inside look at your daily operations.

Virtual Reality in Real Estate

Virtual reality offers immersive experiences that can transform the way potential buyers interact with properties. By leveraging VR technology, real estate agents can provide clients with realistic, 3D property tours that can be accessed from anywhere in the world.

VR Property Tours

Creating virtual reality property tours allows potential buyers to explore properties in-depth without physically being present. This can save time and resources for both agents and clients, particularly when dealing with long-distance or international buyers.

Virtual Staging

Virtual staging allows real estate agents to digitally furnish and decorate properties, making them more appealing to potential buyers. This cost-effective alternative to traditional staging can help clients visualize the potential of a space and generate more interest in a listing.

VR Conferencing

Virtual reality conferencing tools, such as Spatial and AltspaceVR, enable real estate agents to meet with clients and colleagues in immersive virtual environments. These platforms can be used for property presentations, negotiations, and networking events, offering a unique and engaging way to conduct business.

Implementing Live Streaming and Virtual Reality

Choose the Right Platforms

Before incorporating live streaming and virtual reality into your marketing strategy, research the various platforms available and choose the ones that best suit your needs and target audience.

Invest in Quality Equipment

To deliver professional, high-quality live streams and VR experiences, invest in the necessary equipment, such as a reliable camera, microphone, and VR headset.

Promote Your Live Streams and VR Content

Promote your live streams and VR content across your social media channels, website, and email marketing campaigns to ensure your audience is aware of these offerings.

Monitor Engagement and Adjust Your Strategy

Track engagement metrics, such as views, comments, and shares, to gauge the effectiveness of your live streaming and VR efforts. Use this data to refine your approach and optimize your content for better results.

In conclusion, live streaming and virtual reality are transformative technologies that offer unique opportunities for real estate agents to connect with their audience and showcase properties. By staying informed about the latest developments, investing in the necessary equipment, and optimizing your content, you can capitalize on the potential of these innovations to grow your business and deliver an enhanced experience for your clients. Embrace these technologies and adapt your marketing strategies to stay ahead of the competition and provide exceptional service in the ever-evolving real estate landscape.

CHAPTER 59:

LEGAL AND ETHICAL CONSIDERATIONS

In the digital age, real estate agents must not only focus on leveraging social media platforms to grow their business but also remain aware of the legal and ethical considerations that come with using these channels. This chapter will discuss some of the most important legal and ethical aspects to consider when using social media as a real estate agent, including privacy, intellectual property, advertising regulations, and professional conduct.

Privacy and Data Protection

When using social media platforms, it is crucial to respect the privacy of your clients and followers. Ensure that you have the necessary permissions to share personal information, photographs, or any other sensitive data related to your clients or their properties. Familiarize yourself with the privacy policies of each platform you use and adhere to the applicable data protection regulations, such as the General Data Protection Regulation (GDPR) in the European Union.

Intellectual Property

Respect the intellectual property rights of others by not using copyrighted material without permission. This includes images, videos, music, and other content. When sharing third-party content, always give proper credit to the original creator and follow any applicable attribution guidelines.

Truthful Advertising and Disclosure

Ensure that your advertising and promotional materials on social media are truthful and not misleading. Avoid making exaggerated or false claims about the properties you represent or the services you offer. Be transparent about any affiliations, partnerships, or paid promotions, and follow the advertising regulations set forth by the relevant real estate governing bodies and the Federal Trade Commission (FTC) in the United States.

Professional Conduct and Ethics

Maintain a high standard of professionalism and ethical conduct when using social media. Avoid engaging in defamatory, discriminatory, or offensive behavior that could harm your reputation or that of your clients. Be respectful of your competitors and refrain from making negative or derogatory comments about them.

Fair Housing Laws

As a real estate agent, it is essential to comply with fair housing laws when using social media for marketing and promotion. Avoid making statements or sharing content that could be perceived as discriminatory based on race, color, religion, sex, handicap, familial status, or national origin. Familiarize yourself with the Fair Housing Act in the United States or equivalent legislation in your jurisdiction to ensure compliance.

Staying Informed and Up-to-Date

Laws and regulations related to social media usage, privacy, and advertising are constantly evolving. Stay informed about the latest developments and updates to ensure you are always operating within the legal and ethical boundaries. Attend workshops, webinars, or conferences, and consult with legal and compliance experts when necessary.

Using social media as a real estate agent offers numerous opportunities to grow your business and connect with clients. However, it is crucial to remain aware of the legal and ethical considerations involved. By respecting privacy, intellectual property rights, advertising regulations, and maintaining a high standard of professional conduct, you can harness the power of social media while minimizing potential risks and ensuring compliance with the law.

CHAPTER 60:

COPYRIGHT AND INTELLECTUAL PROPERTY

As a real estate agent using social media to promote your business, it is vital to understand and respect copyright and intellectual property (IP) rights. This chapter will delve into the key concepts related to copyright and IP, providing guidance on how to use and share content ethically and legally on social media platforms.

What is Intellectual Property?

Intellectual property refers to the creations of the mind, such as inventions, artistic works, designs, and symbols. IP rights protect the interests of creators by granting them exclusive rights over the use and distribution of their creations. The primary types of intellectual property protection are copyright, trademarks, and patents.

Understanding Copyright

Copyright protects original works of authorship, including literary, dramatic, musical, artistic, and certain other intellectual works. In the context of social media, this includes written content, images, videos, music, and other creative materials. Copyright protection is automatic, meaning that a work is protected as soon as it is created and fixed in a tangible form.

Fair Use and Exceptions

The concept of fair use allows for limited use of copyrighted material without permission from the copyright holder, under certain circumstances. Factors considered when determining fair use include the purpose and character of the use, the nature of the copyrighted work, the amount and substantiality of the portion used, and the effect of the use on the potential market for or value of the copyrighted work. It is essential to understand that fair use is a complex legal concept and should not be relied upon without seeking expert advice.

Proper Attribution and Sharing

When sharing content on social media, always credit the original creator and provide a link to the source whenever possible. This not only demonstrates respect for the creator's rights but also helps to build trust and credibility with your audience.

Licensing and Permissions

In some cases, you may need to obtain permission or a license to use copyrighted material. This can include purchasing stock images or music for your content or securing permission from the original creator. Ensure that you understand and comply with the terms of any licenses you acquire, including restrictions on use, modifications, and attribution requirements.

User-Generated Content

Sharing user-generated content (UGC), such as reviews, testimonials, or images featuring your clients' properties, can be an effective marketing strategy. However, it is crucial to obtain the necessary permissions from the creators before sharing their content. In some cases, a simple request for permission may suffice, while in others, a more formal written agreement may be necessary.

Protecting Your Own Intellectual Property

As a real estate agent, you may also create original content for your social media channels. To protect your IP rights, consider registering your copyright, trademark, or patent, as applicable. Additionally, clearly state your ownership and usage terms on your website and social media profiles to deter unauthorized use.

Respecting copyright and intellectual property rights is essential for real estate agents using social media platforms to grow their business. By understanding the key concepts and ensuring that you have the necessary permissions to use and share content, you can maintain an ethical and legally compliant online presence while fostering strong relationships with your clients and audience.

CHAPTER 61:

INDUSTRY REGULATIONS

As a real estate agent using social media to promote your business, it is crucial to be aware of and comply with the various industry regulations governing your profession. This chapter will outline some of the key regulations you should be familiar with to ensure your social media activities adhere to legal and ethical standards.

Real Estate Licensing Laws

Real estate licensing laws regulate the activities of real estate agents and brokers. These laws vary by state or country, so it is essential to familiarize yourself with the specific regulations in your jurisdiction. In general, these laws require real estate professionals to be licensed, maintain continuing education requirements, and adhere to certain ethical standards.

Fair Housing Laws

Fair housing laws protect against discrimination in housing transactions, including renting, buying, and financing. In the United States, the Fair Housing Act prohibits discrimination based on race, color, national origin, religion, sex, familial status, or disability. As a real estate agent, it is essential to ensure that your social media content and advertising do not discriminate against any protected class or otherwise violate fair housing laws.

Real Estate Advertising Regulations

Real estate advertising is subject to a variety of regulations aimed at ensuring accuracy, transparency, and consumer protection. These regulations may include requirements to disclose your real estate agent or broker license information, include specific disclaimers, and avoid false or misleading statements. Be aware of the advertising regulations applicable to your jurisdiction and ensure that your social media content complies with these requirements.

CAN-SPAM Act and Other Email Marketing Regulations

If you use email marketing in conjunction with your social media efforts, be aware of the regulations governing commercial email, such as the CAN-SPAM Act in the United States. These regulations generally require that commercial emails contain accurate header and subject lines, provide a valid physical postal address, and include a clear and conspicuous opt-out mechanism.

Fair Housing Laws

Fair housing laws protect against discrimination in housing transactions, including renting, buying, and financing. In the United States, the Fair Housing Act prohibits discrimination based on race, color, national origin, religion, sex, familial status, or disability. As a real estate agent, it is essential to ensure that your social media content and advertising do not discriminate against any protected class or otherwise violate fair housing laws.

Real Estate Advertising Regulations

Real estate advertising is subject to a variety of regulations aimed at ensuring accuracy, transparency, and consumer protection. These regulations may include requirements to disclose your real estate agent or broker license information, include specific disclaimers, and avoid false or misleading statements. Be aware of the advertising regulations applicable to your jurisdiction and ensure that your social media content complies with these requirements.

CAN-SPAM Act and Other Email Marketing Regulations

If you use email marketing in conjunction with your social media efforts, be aware of the regulations governing commercial email, such as the CAN-SPAM Act in the United States. These regulations generally require that commercial emails contain accurate header and subject lines, provide a valid physical postal address, and include a clear and conspicuous opt-out mechanism.

Privacy Laws and Data Protection

Privacy laws and data protection regulations, such as the General Data Protection Regulation (GDPR) in the European Union or the California Consumer Privacy Act (CCPA) in the United States, govern the collection, use, and disclosure of personal information. Be transparent about your data collection practices, obtain the necessary consents, and implement appropriate security measures to protect the personal information of your clients and followers.

Social Media Platform Policies

In addition to industry-specific regulations, be aware of the policies and guidelines of the social media platforms you use. These policies often address issues such as advertising, prohibited content, and intellectual property rights. Failure to comply with platform policies can result in account suspension or other penalties.

Professional Association Guidelines

Real estate professionals may also be subject to guidelines and ethical standards established by industry associations, such as the National Association of REALTORS® (NAR) in the United States. These guidelines can provide additional guidance on best practices for social media use and other aspects of your real estate business.

Understanding and complying with industry regulations is essential for real estate agents using social media to grow their business. By familiarizing yourself with the relevant laws, platform policies, and professional association guidelines, you can maintain a legally compliant and ethically responsible online presence that supports your professional growth and success.

CHAPTER 62:

MAINTAINING CLIENT CONFIDENTIALITY

In the real estate industry, maintaining client confidentiality is of utmost importance. Real estate agents have a legal and ethical responsibility to protect the sensitive information of their clients. In this chapter, we will discuss how to maintain client confidentiality when using social media and other online platforms to promote your real estate business.

Understanding Confidential Information

Confidential information refers to any data or details about your clients that should not be disclosed without their consent. This can include personal information, financial details, and specifics about a client's property or transaction. As a real estate agent, you must be vigilant about protecting this information and ensuring it is not inadvertently shared on social media or other digital channels.

Establishing and Communicating Privacy Policies

It is essential to have clear privacy policies in place that outline how you collect, store, and share client information. Make sure your clients are aware of these policies and obtain their consent when necessary. Communicate your commitment to protecting client confidentiality on your website, social media profiles, and other marketing materials.

Securely Storing Client Information

Take appropriate measures to secure the storage of client information, both digitally and physically. Use password-protected devices and encrypted storage solutions to protect digital files. Keep physical files locked away when not in use and ensure they are disposed of securely when no longer needed.

Limiting Access to Client Information

Only grant access to client information to individuals who need it to perform their job duties. Keep your team members informed about the importance of maintaining client confidentiality and provide regular training on best practices for handling sensitive information.

Careful Sharing of Information on Social Media

When sharing content on social media, be mindful of any information that could potentially compromise client confidentiality.

Avoid posting specific details about transactions, client names, or personal information without explicit consent. When sharing images of properties, ensure that they do not inadvertently reveal confidential information or invade the privacy of your clients.

Obtaining Consent for Testimonials and Case Studies

Before sharing testimonials or case studies on social media or other marketing channels, obtain written consent from your clients. Ensure they understand how their information will be used and provide them with the option to remain anonymous if desired

Responding to Inquiries and Comments

When engaging with followers on social media, be cautious about disclosing confidential information in your responses to questions or comments. If a follower inquires about specific details regarding a client or transaction, direct them to a private conversation or recommend they contact you directly for more information.

Monitoring and Auditing Social Media Activity

Regularly review your social media activity to ensure that you and your team are not inadvertently sharing confidential information. Implement internal audits and engage in ongoing training to maintain a high level of awareness and compliance with client confidentiality standards.

Maintaining client confidentiality is a critical aspect of building trust and credibility in the real estate industry. By implementing robust privacy policies, securely storing client information, and carefully managing your social media presence, you can protect your clients' sensitive data and uphold your professional reputation.

CHAPTER 63:

TIPS AND ADVICE FOR REAL ESTATE AGENTS

In this chapter, we will provide practical tips and advice for real estate agents who want to harness the power of social media effectively. From staying organized to building meaningful connections, these strategies will help you enhance your online presence and grow your real estate business.

Stay Organized and Consistent

A successful social media presence requires consistency and organization. Use scheduling tools and content calendars to plan your social media posts in advance, ensuring you maintain a regular posting schedule. This will help you stay top-of-mind with your audience and build a loyal following.

Be Authentic and Approachable

Your online presence should reflect your unique personality and expertise.

Be genuine and approachable in your social media interactions, showcasing your knowledge and passion for the real estate industry. This will help you build trust and rapport with your audience.

Engage with Your Audience

To build a strong online community, make an effort to engage with your audience regularly. Respond to comments and messages promptly, and take the time to acknowledge and interact with your followers. This will demonstrate that you value their input and help foster meaningful connections.

Utilize Video Content

Video content is highly engaging and can be an effective way to showcase properties, share market updates, and provide valuable insights. Leverage video on platforms like YouTube, Instagram, and TikTok to reach new audiences and diversify your content strategy.

Leverage Local Hashtags and Geotags

To increase your visibility and connect with potential clients in your area, use local hashtags and geotags in your social media posts. This will help you tap into relevant conversations and establish yourself as a knowledgeable, local resource.

Collaborate with Industry Professionals

Partner with other professionals in the real estate industry, such as mortgage brokers, interior designers, and home inspectors, to create valuable content and expand your reach. These collaborations can help you provide additional value to your audience and strengthen your professional network.

Keep Up with Industry Trends

Stay informed about emerging trends and changes in the real estate market. Share your insights and analysis with your audience to position yourself as a thought leader and trusted resource.

Offer Value-Driven Content

Focus on providing valuable, informative content that helps your audience make informed decisions about buying or selling property. This will not only demonstrate your expertise but also help you build a reputation as a trusted source of information.

Track and Analyze Your Performance

Regularly monitor your social media analytics to measure the effectiveness of your efforts. Use this data to refine your strategies and make informed decisions about where to invest your time and resources.

Invest in Continued Learning

The digital landscape is constantly evolving, and staying up-to-date with the latest tools, platforms, and strategies is crucial to your success. Invest in continued learning to ensure you remain at the forefront of social media marketing in the real estate industry.

By implementing these tips and strategies, real estate agents can harness the power of social media to grow their business and build a strong online presence. Stay organized, authentic, and engaged with your audience, and continue to learn and adapt to the ever-changing world of social media marketing.

CHAPTER 64:

STAYING MOTIVATED

In the fast-paced and highly competitive world of real estate, staying motivated can be challenging. This chapter will provide you with actionable strategies and advice for maintaining motivation and resilience as you navigate the dynamic landscape of social media marketing for your real estate business.

Set Clear Goals and Objectives

Having well-defined goals and objectives will help you stay focused on your priorities and maintain a sense of purpose. Regularly review and adjust your goals to ensure they remain relevant, achievable, and aligned with your overall business objectives.

Celebrate Small Wins

Take the time to recognize and celebrate your achievements, both big and small.

By acknowledging your progress and rewarding yourself for the hard work you put in, you'll be more motivated to continue moving forward.

Stay Connected with Your Community

Cultivate strong relationships with fellow real estate professionals, industry experts, and your online audience. By staying connected with others who share your passion and dedication, you'll be better equipped to overcome challenges and maintain your motivation.

Embrace Continued Learning

Invest in your professional development by staying up-to-date with industry trends, attending workshops, and learning from industry leaders. Embrace a growth mindset and view challenges as opportunities to learn and improve.

Manage Your Time Effectively

Effective time management is essential for maintaining motivation and preventing burnout. Develop a routine that allows you to allocate sufficient time to your most important tasks and prioritize self-care and relaxation.

Maintain a Positive Mindset

Focus on cultivating a positive mindset by celebrating your successes, staying optimistic about the future, and surrounding yourself with supportive, like-minded individuals. A positive attitude can help you stay motivated even during challenging times.

Seek Feedback and Constructive Criticism

Embrace feedback and constructive criticism from your peers, mentors, and audience. Use this feedback to learn and grow, and view it as an opportunity to refine your strategies and improve your skills.

Reflect on Your Progress

Regularly reflect on your progress and the milestones you've achieved in your real estate career. Use these reflections to remind yourself of how far you've come and to fuel your motivation for continued growth and success.

Stay Flexible and Adaptable

The world of social media and real estate is constantly evolving. Stay open to change and be prepared to pivot your strategies when necessary. Embrace new challenges and view them as opportunities to innovate and grow your business.

Find Your "Why"

Reconnect with the core reasons behind your passion for real estate and social media marketing. By understanding and staying connected to your "why," you'll be more resilient and motivated to overcome obstacles and achieve success.

Staying motivated as a real estate agent in the world of social media marketing requires a combination of goal-setting, celebration, connection, learning, time management, and adaptability. By implementing these strategies, you'll be better equipped to maintain motivation and continue to thrive in your real estate career.

CHAPTER 65:

TIME MANAGEMENT

Effective time management is essential for real estate agents looking to successfully leverage social media to grow their businesses. Balancing the demands of social media marketing with the day-to-day responsibilities of managing properties and working with clients can be challenging. This chapter will provide you with practical strategies and tools to help you manage your time more efficiently and maximize your productivity.

Prioritize Your Tasks

Learn to prioritize your tasks based on their importance and urgency. Use tools like the Eisenhower Matrix to help you categorize tasks into four quadrants: urgent and important, important but not urgent, urgent but not important, and not urgent or important. Focus on completing tasks in the urgent and important quadrant first, followed by the important but not urgent tasks.

Set SMART Goals

Ensure your goals are Specific, Measurable, Achievable, Relevant, and Time-bound (SMART). SMART goals provide a clear and actionable roadmap for success, allowing you to better allocate your time and resources.

Create a Daily Schedule

Develop a daily schedule that allocates time for both your social media marketing efforts and your core real estate responsibilities. Be realistic about the time each task requires and build in buffer time for unexpected interruptions or delays.

Break Tasks into Smaller Steps

Breaking larger tasks into smaller, more manageable steps can make them feel less overwhelming and easier to tackle. This approach can help you maintain momentum and motivation while working towards your larger objectives.

Use Time Management Tools

Leverage time management tools, such as digital calendars, to-do lists, and project management software, to help you stay organized, prioritize tasks, and track your progress. These tools can also help you identify areas where you may be spending too much or too little time.

Delegate and Outsource

Identify tasks that can be delegated to team members or outsourced to external service providers. This will enable you to focus on your highest priority tasks and maximize your productivity.

Set Boundaries

Establish clear boundaries between your work and personal life. Schedule dedicated time for self-care and relaxation, and avoid the temptation to work outside of your designated working hours.

Implement the Pomodoro Technique

The Pomodoro Technique is a time management method that involves breaking your work into short, focused intervals (typically 25 minutes) called "Pomodoros," followed by a short break. This technique can help you maintain focus, reduce burnout, and increase productivity.

Monitor and Adjust

Regularly assess your time management practices to identify areas for improvement. Make adjustments as needed to optimize your productivity and ensure you're allocating your time effectively.

Effective time management is a critical skill for real estate agents looking to succeed in the world of social media marketing. By prioritizing tasks, setting SMART goals, creating a daily schedule, breaking tasks into smaller steps, utilizing time management tools, delegating, setting boundaries, implementing the Pomodoro Technique, and monitoring your progress, you'll be better equipped to maximize your productivity and achieve your goals.

CHAPTER 66:

OVERCOMING COMMON CHALLENGES

Real estate agents face various challenges when incorporating social media into their marketing strategies. This chapter will explore common obstacles and provide practical advice on how to overcome them, ensuring your social media efforts yield positive results.

Limited Time and Resources

Challenge: Many agents struggle to balance their social media marketing efforts with their day-to-day responsibilities. Solution: Develop a time management plan, prioritize tasks, and consider delegating or outsourcing certain activities. Utilize scheduling tools and content repurposing strategies to maximize efficiency.

Keeping Up with Platform Changes

Challenge: Social media platforms frequently update their features, algorithms, and policies, making it difficult for agents to stay current.
Solution: Dedicate time to staying informed about industry news and platform updates. Join relevant online communities, subscribe to industry blogs, and participate in webinars to keep your knowledge up-to-date.

Generating High-Quality Content

Challenge: Creating engaging and valuable content consistently can be challenging.
Solution: Develop a content strategy, brainstorm ideas, and create a content calendar to plan ahead. Utilize various content formats (e.g., images, videos, articles) and seek inspiration from successful real estate professionals.

Maintaining Consistency

Challenge: Maintaining a consistent posting schedule and brand identity can be difficult.
Solution: Establish a posting schedule, set content themes, and develop a brand voice and visual identity to create a cohesive online presence. Use scheduling tools to automate content publishing.

Building an Engaged Audience

Challenge: Attracting and retaining an engaged audience can be challenging.
Solution: Focus on providing value to your target audience through informative, entertaining, and shareable content. Encourage engagement through calls-to-action, responding to comments, and participating in relevant online communities.

Measuring Success

Challenge: Quantifying the success of your social media efforts can be complex.
Solution: Identify key performance indicators (KPIs) relevant to your objectives, track them consistently, and analyze data to make informed decisions. Utilize social media analytics tools to streamline this process.

Navigating Legal and Ethical Considerations

Challenge: Ensuring compliance with industry regulations, copyright laws, and maintaining client confidentiality is crucial.
Solution: Familiarize yourself with relevant laws and regulations, consult legal experts when necessary, and implement best practices to protect your business and clients.

Staying Motivated

Challenge: Maintaining motivation and persistence in the face of challenges is essential for long-term success.
Solution: Set realistic goals, celebrate small victories, and seek support from peers or mentors. Continuously learn and adapt to maintain motivation and stay ahead of the competition.

Overcoming common challenges faced by real estate agents in their social media marketing efforts is critical for success. By addressing these obstacles head-on and implementing practical solutions, you can ensure your social media strategy remains effective and drives positive results for your business.

CHAPTER 67:

GRAPHIC DESIGN TOOLS

Creating visually appealing content is essential for capturing the attention of your audience and improving the overall impact of your social media marketing efforts. This chapter will discuss the importance of graphic design tools, focusing on Canva.com and other easy-to-use alternatives to help you create stunning visuals for your real estate business.

The Importance of Graphic Design Tools

Compelling visuals are crucial for capturing your audience's attention and conveying your brand message effectively. Graphic design tools enable real estate agents to create professional-quality images, videos, and other media assets without requiring advanced design skills or software knowledge.

Canva.com: A Comprehensive Design Solution

Canva is an online graphic design platform that offers a user-friendly interface and a vast library of templates, fonts, images, and other design elements. It allows you to create various types of content, such as social media posts, advertisements, brochures, and more. Canva also offers collaboration features, allowing multiple team members to work on a design project simultaneously.

Key Features of Canva

- **Drag-and-drop editor:** Canva's intuitive editor allows you to easily customize templates and design elements with a few clicks.
- **Extensive template library:** Canva offers thousands of professionally-designed templates for various content types and industries, making it easy to create on-brand visuals.
- **Stock images and icons:** Access a large collection of high-quality stock images, icons, and illustrations to enhance your designs.
- **Custom fonts and colors:** Customize your designs with a variety of fonts and colors to match your brand identity.
- **Collaboration tools:** Work with team members to create and edit designs in real-time, streamlining the design process.

Other Graphic Design Tools

While Canva is an excellent choice for most real estate agents, there are other graphic design tools available that may better suit your needs:

- **Adobe Spark:** A simple online design tool that offers templates and customization options for creating social media posts, videos, and web pages.

- Crello: A design platform with a large library of templates, animations, and other design elements for creating engaging visual content.
- Snappa: A graphic design tool with a focus on social media graphics, offering templates, stock images, and collaboration features.
- Piktochart: A design tool specifically tailored for creating infographics, presentations, and reports, making it ideal for presenting data-driven content.

Choosing the Right Tool for Your Needs

Consider your specific requirements when selecting a graphic design tool, including:
- Ease of use: Select a tool that is user-friendly and does not require advanced design skills.
- Templates and design elements: Look for a tool with a wide range of templates and design elements that cater to the real estate industry.
- Customization options: Ensure the tool offers sufficient customization options to create on-brand visuals.
- Pricing: Compare pricing plans and choose a tool that fits within your budget.
- Collaboration features: If you work with a team, select a tool that offers collaboration and file-sharing capabilities.

Graphic design tools, such as Canva.com, are invaluable for real estate agents looking to create visually appealing content for their social media marketing efforts.

By selecting a user-friendly design platform that offers a range of templates and customization options, you can produce professional-quality visuals that effectively convey your brand message and engage your audience.

CHAPTER 68:

STOCK IMAGE RESOURCES

High-quality visuals are essential for creating engaging social media content that captures your audience's attention and reinforces your real estate brand. Stock image resources, such as Unsplash.com and Shutterstock.com, provide a vast library of photos and illustrations that can be used to enhance your content. This chapter will discuss the benefits of using stock image resources and provide an overview of these two popular platforms.

The Importance of Stock Image Resources

Using professional, high-quality images in your social media content is crucial for conveying your brand's credibility and professionalism. Stock image resources provide a cost-effective and time-saving solution for sourcing visually appealing images that can be incorporated into your content.

Benefits of using stock image resources include:
- Access to a vast library of images: Stock image websites offer millions of images, covering a wide range of topics and styles.
- Time and cost savings: Save time and effort searching for the perfect image, and avoid the costs associated with hiring a professional photographer or purchasing individual images.
- Legal usage: Stock image resources provide licensing options that ensure you can use the images in your content without violating copyright laws.

Unsplash.com

Unsplash is a popular stock image resource that offers a vast library of high-resolution images, free for personal and commercial use. Unsplash's collection is contributed by a global community of photographers, ensuring a diverse range of styles and subjects.

Key features of Unsplash.com:
- Free to use: Unsplash's images are available under the Unsplash License, which allows for free use in personal and commercial projects.
- High-resolution images: Unsplash offers high-quality images that can be used for digital and print media.
- User-friendly search: Easily find images by searching keywords or browsing through curated collections.
- Regular updates: New images are added to Unsplash's library regularly, ensuring a fresh selection of visuals for your content.

Shutterstock.com

Shutterstock is a well-known stock image resource that offers a massive library of royalty-free images, illustrations, and vectors. With a focus on professional and high-quality visuals, Shutterstock is an excellent resource for real estate agents seeking images for their social media content and marketing materials.

Key features of Shutterstock.com:
- Extensive library: Shutterstock boasts an impressive collection of over 350 million images, illustrations, and vectors.
- Royalty-free licensing: Shutterstock offers various licensing options, allowing you to use the images in your content without worrying about copyright infringement.
- Advanced search capabilities: Find the perfect image quickly and easily using Shutterstock's advanced search features, including filters and keyword suggestions.
- Subscription plans: Shutterstock offers flexible subscription plans that cater to different usage needs and budgets.

Choosing the Right Stock Image Resource

When selecting a stock image resource, consider the following factors:
- Image quality: Ensure the resource offers high-quality images that align with your brand's visual identity.
- Licensing options: Verify that the licensing options provided by the resource allow for legal use in your content and marketing materials.

- Ease of use: Choose a resource with a user-friendly interface and search capabilities, making it easy to find the images you need.
- Budget: Compare the costs of different stock image resources and select the one that best suits your budget and usage needs.

Stock image resources, such as Unsplash.com and Shutterstock.com, offer real estate agents a convenient and cost-effective solution for sourcing high-quality visuals for their social media content and marketing materials. By selecting a stock image resource that provides a diverse range of images and licensing options, you can enhance your content and reinforce your brand's professionalism and credibility.

CHAPTER 69:

VIDEO EDITING TOOLS

Video content is a powerful tool for real estate agents to showcase properties, provide virtual tours, and offer valuable insights into the real estate market. To create engaging and professional-looking videos, it's essential to use video editing tools that simplify the process and enhance your content. This chapter will discuss some popular video editing tools and their key features, helping you choose the right one for your needs.

Adobe Premiere Pro

Adobe Premiere Pro is a widely-used, professional video editing software suitable for real estate agents looking to create high-quality videos. With its comprehensive set of features, Adobe Premiere Pro allows for advanced video editing, including color grading, motion graphics integration, and audio editing.

Key features of Adobe Premiere Pro:
- Non-linear editing: Arrange and manipulate video clips in any order on the timeline without affecting the original source material.
- Extensive file format support: Import and export a wide range of video and audio file formats.
- Integration with other Adobe Creative Cloud applications: Seamlessly collaborate with other Adobe software, such as Adobe After Effects, Adobe Photoshop, and Adobe Audition.
- Regular updates and improvements: Adobe consistently adds new features and enhancements to Premiere Pro, ensuring you stay up-to-date with the latest video editing trends and technologies.

Final Cut Pro

Final Cut Pro is a professional video editing software developed by Apple Inc., specifically designed for Mac users. It offers a user-friendly interface and powerful editing features that make it suitable for real estate agents of varying skill levels.

Key features of Final Cut Pro:
- Magnetic Timeline: Easily arrange and edit video clips on the timeline, which automatically adjusts to accommodate changes.
- Multicam editing: Sync and edit footage from multiple camera angles simultaneously.

- Advanced color grading and correction: Enhance your videos with professional color grading tools and LUT support.
- Integration with Apple ecosystem: Seamlessly work with other Apple applications, such as Motion and Compressor, for additional functionality.

DaVinci Resolve

DaVinci Resolve is a professional video editing software that combines editing, color grading, visual effects, and audio post-production in a single application. With its comprehensive feature set and free version available, DaVinci Resolve is a popular choice for real estate agents looking for an affordable yet powerful video editing tool.

Key features of DaVinci Resolve:
- Non-linear editing: Edit video clips on a flexible timeline that allows for precise control over your edits.
- Professional color grading: Achieve high-quality color grading with advanced tools and color management features.
- Fusion visual effects: Create and edit visual effects using the integrated Fusion page.
- Fairlight audio: Access professional audio post-production tools within the software.

iMovie
iMovie is a user-friendly video editing software developed by Apple Inc., specifically designed for Mac and iOS users.

With its intuitive interface and basic editing features, iMovie is an excellent choice for real estate agents new to video editing or looking for a simplified editing process.

Key features of iMovie:
- Drag-and-drop editing: Easily arrange and edit video clips using the straightforward timeline.
- Built-in templates and effects: Access a range of pre-made templates, transitions, and effects to enhance your videos.
- Green screen and picture-in-picture support: Create more dynamic videos with green screen and picture-in-picture effects.
- Integration with Apple ecosystem: Seamlessly work with other Apple applications, such as GarageBand and Photos, and export directly to social media platforms.

Choosing the Right Video Editing Tool

When selecting a video editing tool, consider the following factors:
- Skill level: Choose a video editing tool that matches your skill level and offers the features you require for your content.
- Budget: Compare the costs of different video editing tools, taking into account any subscription fees or one-time purchases.
- Platform compatibility: Ensure the video editing tool you choose is compatible with your operating system and hardware.
- User interface: Select a video editing tool with a user interface that you find intuitive and easy to navigate.

- Integration with other tools: Consider how well the video editing tool integrates with other software or applications you use, such as graphic design tools, audio editing software, or stock image resources.

Tips for Effective Video Editing

To create compelling and professional real estate videos, keep these video editing tips in mind:

- Plan your content: Before you start editing, have a clear idea of your video's purpose, target audience, and desired outcome.
- Maintain a consistent style: Develop a consistent visual and audio style for your real estate videos, which reflects your brand and engages your target audience.
- Keep it concise: Edit your videos to be as concise as possible, removing any unnecessary footage or information. Aim to keep your audience engaged and deliver your message effectively.
- Use transitions and effects wisely: While transitions and effects can enhance your videos, overusing them can be distracting. Use them sparingly and only when they contribute to your video's overall message.
- Focus on storytelling: A well-crafted story can make your real estate videos more engaging and memorable. Use your video editing tools to create a narrative that showcases your property, highlights key features, and connects with your audience.

- Prioritize audio quality: Ensure your videos have clear and consistent audio, as poor audio quality can detract from the overall viewing experience.
- Continuously learn and improve: As you gain experience with video editing tools, continue to learn new techniques and refine your skills to create more effective and engaging real estate videos.

In conclusion, choosing the right video editing tool is essential for creating professional and engaging real estate videos. By considering your skill level, budget, platform compatibility, and desired features, you can select the most suitable video editing software to enhance your real estate marketing efforts. Additionally, implementing effective video editing techniques can help you create compelling and memorable content that connects with your target audience and drives results.

CHAPTER 70:

100 SOCIAL MEDIA POST IDEAS

As a real estate agent, having a steady stream of engaging social media content is essential for building your brand and connecting with your audience. Here are 100 unique post ideas to inspire your next social media updates on YouTube, Facebook, Instagram, or Pinterest:

- Share a sneak peek of an upcoming property listing with a teaser photo.
- Host a live Q&A session answering common questions about the home-buying process.
- Share a personal story about why you became a real estate agent.
- Highlight a local business or community event in your area.
- Create an infographic with helpful tips for homebuyers or sellers.
- Share a success story of a client finding their dream home.
- Post a poll asking your followers about their favorite home features.

- Share a before-and-after transformation of a staged property.
- Offer expert advice on how to prepare a home for sale.
- Create a short video explaining different mortgage types.
- Share a series of photos showcasing a unique architectural feature in a property.
- Post a quote from a satisfied client.
- Share a photo from a recent open house event.
- Post a video tour of a luxurious property.
- Share your top tips for increasing a home's curb appeal.
- Highlight the benefits of working with a real estate agent.
- Share a fun fact about the history of a local neighborhood.
- Create a "Did You Know?" post about a unique aspect of your local real estate market.
- Showcase a stunning interior design detail from a listed property.
- Post a throwback photo of a previously sold property.
- Share an article about the latest real estate market trends.
- Post a photo of a property with a breathtaking view.
- Create a "Home of the Week" feature showcasing an exceptional listing.
- Share a video explaining the benefits of pre-approval for homebuyers.
- Post a behind-the-scenes look at a property photo shoot.
- Highlight a local charity or community organization you support.
- Share a video discussing the pros and cons of renting vs. buying.
- Create a listicle of the top local attractions in your area.
- Post a photo of a pet-friendly property feature.

- Share a video explaining common real estate terms and jargon.
- Create a post celebrating a recent career milestone or award.
- Share a seasonal home maintenance tip.
- Post a photo of a unique outdoor living space.
- Create a "Meet the Team" feature, introducing your colleagues or support staff.
- Share a video on the benefits of working with a buyer's agent.
- Post a photo showcasing a stunning kitchen or bathroom renovation.
- Share a helpful resource for first-time homebuyers.
- Create a post highlighting the eco-friendly features of a property.
- Share a video discussing common home inspection issues.
- Post a photo of a cozy living room, inviting followers to share their own.
- Share an article about the future of the real estate industry.
- Create a post discussing the advantages of downsizing.
- Share a video tour of a historic property.
- Post a photo of a charming front porch or entryway.
- Share your thoughts on a popular interior design trend.
- Create a post explaining the importance of a property's location.
- Share a video about the process of obtaining a mortgage.
- Post a photo of a beautifully landscaped garden.

- Share an article about tax benefits for homeowners.
- Create a post discussing the impact of interest rates on the real estate market.
- Share a video on how to stage a home for sale.
- Post a photo of a property's unique architectural detail.
- Share an article about the benefits of investing in real estate.
- Create a post about the best schools in your area.
- Share a video discussing the role of a seller's agent.
- Post a photo of a recently closed transaction with happy clients.
- Share a story of how you helped a client overcome a challenge during the home-buying process.
- Create a post discussing the value of home warranties for buyers and sellers.
- Share a video explaining how to choose the right neighborhood for your lifestyle.
- Post a photo of a luxurious master suite or spa-like bathroom.
- Share an article about smart home technology and its impact on real estate.
- Create a post highlighting a unique or unusual property listing.
- Share a video discussing the importance of pricing a home correctly.
- Post a photo of a property's stunning outdoor living area or pool.
- Share a helpful moving checklist for new homeowners.
- Create a post about the benefits of energy-efficient homes.

- Share a video on how to improve your credit score before applying for a mortgage.
- Post a photo of a property's impressive home office or workspace.
- Share an article about the latest home design trends.
- Create a post discussing the process of refinancing a mortgage.
- Share a video on how to negotiate the best deal on a home purchase.
- Post a photo of a unique or quirky property feature.
- Share a local news story related to real estate or housing.
- Create a post about the advantages of investing in a vacation property.
- Share a video discussing common misconceptions about the home-buying process.
- Post a photo of a stylish or well-designed living area.
- Share an article about the future of urban development and its impact on real estate.
- Create a post about the benefits of owning a second home.
- Share a video on the importance of a good credit score when buying a home.
- Post a photo of a property with an amazing backyard or outdoor space.
- Share a local real estate success story or case study.
- Create a post about the perks of living in a walkable neighborhood.
- Share a video discussing the role of a real estate attorney during a transaction.
- Post a photo of a stunning property at sunset or sunrise.

- Share an article about the impact of transportation infrastructure on real estate values.
- Create a post about the challenges and rewards of owning rental properties.
- Share a video on the process of selling a home for the first time.
- Post a photo of a property with an incredible view or unique location.
- Share a list of the most important questions to ask when hiring a real estate agent.
- Create a post about the latest innovations in home construction.
- Share a video discussing the benefits of home staging for sellers.
- Post a photo of a unique or eye-catching piece of home décor.
- Share an article about the role of technology in the real estate industry.
- Create a post about the importance of professional photography in marketing a property.
- Share a video on the benefits of working with a buyer's agent when purchasing a home.
- Post a photo showcasing a property's beautifully landscaped yard or garden.
- Share an article about the process of obtaining a mortgage pre-approval.
- Create a post discussing the value of curb appeal for home sellers.
- Share a video on how to determine the right listing price for a property.

- Post a photo of a well-staged dining room or kitchen, highlighting the importance of presentation.
- Share a list of tips for first-time homebuyers.
- Create a post about the pros and cons of different types of home loans.
- Share a video on how to choose the right real estate agent for your needs.
- Post a photo of a property with unique architectural features or design elements.
- Share an article about the effects of gentrification on local real estate markets.
- Create a post discussing the tax benefits of homeownership.
- Share a video on how to prepare your home for a successful open house.
- Post a photo of a beautifully renovated kitchen or bathroom in a listed property.
- Share a list of the top local schools, parks, or community amenities in your area.
- Create a post about the benefits of downsizing or moving to a smaller home.
- Share a video on the steps involved in closing a real estate transaction.
- Post a photo of a cozy, inviting bedroom in a home for sale.
- Share an article about the importance of a strong online presence for real estate agents.
- Create a post discussing the role of a seller's agent in a real estate transaction.
- Share a video on the process of buying a home at auction.
- Post a photo of a unique or historical property in your area.
- Share a list of home maintenance tips for new homeowners.

- Create a post about the advantages of living in a planned community or development.
- Share a video on how to make your home more eco-friendly and energy-efficient.
- Post a photo of an interesting or unusual architectural detail in a listed property.
- Share an article about the role of a real estate appraiser in the home-buying process.
- Create a post discussing the ins and outs of real estate investment.
- Share a video on how to stage a home on a budget.
- Post a photo of a breathtaking property view or scenic location.
- Share a list of the best local spots for dining, shopping, or entertainment in your area.
- Create a post about the importance of a home inspection for buyers.
- Share a video on the process of applying for a mortgage.
- Post a photo of a beautifully designed outdoor space or patio.
- Share an article about the impact of interest rates on the real estate market.
- Create a post discussing the advantages of hiring a property manager for rental properties.
- Share a video on how to improve a home's resale value through strategic upgrades.
- Post a photo of a charming or character-filled property in your area.
- Share a list of common misconceptions about the home buying process.

- Create a post discussing the benefits of investing in commercial real estate.
- Share a video on the importance of a well-written property description.
- Post a photo of a stunning luxury property or high-end home.
- Share an article about the advantages of purchasing a fixer-upper or distressed property.
- Create a post discussing the role of a title company in a real estate transaction.
- Share a video on how to effectively negotiate a real estate deal.
- Post a photo of a home's unique or hidden storage solutions.
- Share a list of tips for creating an appealing rental property listing.
- Create a post about the impact of technology on the real estate industry.
- Share a video on the benefits of using a virtual tour to showcase a property.
- Post a photo of a property's eye-catching exterior design or color scheme.
- Share an article about the factors that affect property values.
- Create a post discussing the importance of properly pricing a rental property.
- Share a video on how to enhance a property's curb appeal with simple landscaping ideas.
- Post a photo of a home with an incredible outdoor entertainment area or pool.

- Share a list of strategies for marketing a property to potential buyers.
- Create a post about the role of a real estate attorney in the home buying process.
- Share a video on the key differences between a condo, townhouse, and single-family home.
- Post a photo of a property's unique or innovative interior design elements.
- Share an article about the benefits of using a professional photographer for property listings.
- Create a post discussing the importance of networking and relationship building in the real estate industry.
- Share a video on the steps to take when preparing your home for sale.
- Post a photo of a local event, fair, or festival in your community to showcase the area's attractions.

CHAPTER 71:

GET CREATIVE LOCALLY ON SOCIAL MEDIA

Creating posts that focus on local elements of your community can help real estate agents showcase the unique aspects of the area and foster a sense of belonging among potential buyers. Here are some ideas for community-focused social media posts:

- Highlight a local park, hiking trail, or outdoor recreation area that residents enjoy.
- Share a photo or video of a popular local restaurant, café, or bakery, with a brief description of what makes it special.
- Showcase a local community event, such as a farmer's market, street fair, or art festival.
- Share the history or interesting facts about a local landmark, monument, or architectural feature.
- Post a photo or video of a local sports team, school, or community organization, highlighting their accomplishments or activities.
- Share information about upcoming community events, workshops, or classes that might interest your audience.

- Interview a local business owner or community leader, discussing their insights about the community and how it has evolved over time.
- Highlight a local charity or nonprofit organization and the positive impact they have on the community.
- Share a photo or video of a picturesque or unique neighborhood in your area, with a brief description of its features.
- Post a "Did You Know?" fact about your community that might surprise or interest your audience.
- Share a local success story of a business, organization, or individual who has made a positive impact on the community.
- Highlight the benefits of living in your community, such as access to quality schools, healthcare, or public transportation.
- Share a photo or video of a community garden, mural, or other public art installation that adds character to the area.
- Post a "Meet the Neighbors" feature, where you interview local residents about their favorite aspects of the community.
- Share a local news story or announcement that showcases the positive aspects of your area.

These community-focused social media post ideas will help real estate agents connect with their audience on a more personal level and demonstrate their expertise about the local area.

CHAPTER 72:

SOCIAL MEDIA CONTESTS & GIVEAWAYS

Social media contests and giveaways are powerful tools for generating engagement, increasing brand awareness, and expanding your real estate agent network. They not only encourage interaction from your followers but also attract new audiences who might be interested in your services. In this chapter, we will delve into the world of social media contests and giveaways, offering clear and concise instructions, ideas, and best practices for real estate agents to follow.

Types of Social Media Contests & Giveaways:

There are several types of contests and giveaways that you can run on social media platforms. Some popular options include:

- Photo Contests: Participants submit photos related to a specific theme, such as their dream home or favorite local spot.
- Caption Contests: Participants submit witty or creative captions for a photo you provide.

- Trivia Contests: Participants answer questions related to real estate, local history, or the housing market.
- Sweepstakes: Participants enter for a chance to win a prize by simply liking, commenting, or sharing a post.
- Voting Contests: Participants submit entries and encourage their networks to vote for their submission.

Choosing a Contest Theme:

Select a theme for your contest or giveaway that relates to your real estate business and resonates with your target audience. Some theme ideas include:

- Home Improvement: Participants share their favorite DIY home improvement projects.
- Neighborhood Spotlights: Highlight local businesses or attractions and encourage participants to share their experiences.
- Home Staging Tips: Participants share their best home staging tips or before-and-after photos.

Defining Contest Rules & Guidelines:

Clearly outline the rules and guidelines for your contest or giveaway. Include eligibility criteria, entry instructions, submission deadlines, and voting procedures. Be sure to comply with the platform's terms of service and any applicable laws and regulations.

Selecting a Prize:

Choose a prize that is relevant to your real estate business and valuable to your target audience. Some prize ideas include:
- Gift cards to local businesses or home improvement stores
- Complimentary home staging or interior design consultation
- Free home evaluation or market analysis

Promoting Your Contest or Giveaway:

Promote your contest or giveaway across all your social media channels, email marketing campaigns, and website. Use eye-catching graphics and compelling copy to encourage participation. You can also collaborate with local businesses, influencers, or media outlets to boost visibility.

Managing & Monitoring Contest Submissions:

Keep track of contest submissions, engage with participants, and provide regular updates on the contest's progress. Use a consistent hashtag for easy tracking and consider using a third-party contest management tool to simplify the process.

Announcing & Celebrating Winners:

Once your contest or giveaway has ended, promptly announce the winner(s) on your social media channels. Showcase their submissions, celebrate their achievements, and thank all participants for their involvement. Be sure to deliver the prize(s) as promised and consider sharing a follow-up story or testimonial from the winner(s).

By incorporating social media contests and giveaways into your marketing strategy, you can create buzz around your real estate business, strengthen your online presence, and foster a sense of community among your followers.

CHAPTER 73:

SOCIAL MEDIA & SEO

Social media and search engine optimization (SEO) are two essential components of a successful digital marketing strategy for real estate agents. While they may seem like separate entities, they often work together to drive traffic, increase brand visibility, and generate leads. In this chapter, we will explore the relationship between social media and SEO, offering tips and best practices for real estate agents looking to harness the power of these two channels.

Understanding the Connection Between Social Media & SEO

Social media platforms and search engines both serve as discovery tools for users searching for information, products, or services. While social media focuses on creating and sharing content to engage users, SEO aims to improve the visibility of your website on search engine result pages (SERPs). The two can work hand-in-hand to complement each other and strengthen your overall digital marketing efforts.

Social Media's Impact on SEO

While social media may not have a direct impact on search engine rankings, it can still influence your SEO efforts in several ways:

- Driving Traffic: Social media can drive traffic to your website, which can signal to search engines that your content is valuable and relevant.
- Building Authority: A strong social media presence can help establish your brand as an authority in the real estate industry, which can improve your website's credibility and search engine rankings.
- Enhancing Content Visibility: Sharing content on social media can lead to more backlinks and mentions, which can boost your website's SEO performance.
- Improving User Engagement: Social media can foster user engagement, which can lead to longer dwell times and lower bounce rates on your website.

Optimizing Your Social Media Profiles for SEO

To maximize the SEO benefits of your social media presence, consider the following tips:

- Complete Your Profile: Fill out all profile information fields, including your business name, contact information, and website URL, to improve visibility and credibility.
- Use Keywords: Incorporate relevant keywords in your profile bio and post descriptions to enhance discoverability and search engine indexing.

- Include Links: Add links to your website and other social media profiles to create a strong network of interconnected channels.

Creating Shareable Content

Producing high-quality, shareable content is crucial to leveraging the power of social media for SEO. Consider these tips when creating content:

- Be Valuable: Provide content that offers real value to your audience, such as market insights, home buying tips, or community spotlights.
- Be Engaging: Craft content that encourages engagement, such as asking questions, sharing stories, or hosting live Q&A sessions.
- Be Visual: Use eye-catching images, videos, and infographics to capture your audience's attention and encourage sharing.
- Be Consistent: Post regularly and maintain a consistent tone, style, and message to build trust and credibility.

Encouraging Social Sharing & Engagement

To increase the likelihood of your content being shared, follow these guidelines:

- Use Social Sharing Buttons: Make it easy for users to share your content by including social sharing buttons on your website and blog posts.

- Engage with Your Audience: Respond to comments, answer questions, and show appreciation for user-generated content to foster a sense of community.
- Leverage Influencers & Partners: Collaborate with local influencers or industry partners to expand your reach and increase the chances of your content being shared.

Tracking Social Media & SEO Performance

Monitor your social media and SEO performance using analytics tools, such as Google Analytics and platform-specific insights. Key metrics to track include:
- Website Traffic: Measure the volume of traffic coming from social media channels.
- Engagement Rates: Track likes, comments, shares, and other forms of user engagement.
- Bounce Rates & Dwell Time: Analyze how long users are spending on your website after arriving from social media channels and the bounce rate, which indicates the percentage of users who leave without further engagement.

Integrating Social Media & SEO Strategies

To make the most of your social media and SEO efforts, consider integrating the two strategies:
- Coordinate Content: Align your social media and website content to reinforce your brand messaging and create a cohesive user experience.

- Cross-Promote: Share your website content on social media platforms and vice versa to reach a wider audience and drive traffic between channels.
- Leverage Hashtags: Use relevant hashtags on social media to enhance content discoverability and connect with users interested in real estate topics.
- Utilize Local SEO: Combine your social media efforts with local SEO strategies, such as optimizing your Google My Business listing and using location-specific keywords, to target potential clients in your service area.

By understanding the connection between social media and SEO, real estate agents can harness the power of both channels to increase brand visibility, drive website traffic, and generate leads. By optimizing your social media profiles, creating shareable content, and integrating social media and SEO strategies, you can elevate your digital marketing efforts and achieve greater success in the competitive real estate industry.

CHAPTER 74:

SOCIAL MEDIA CHALLENGES

Social media challenges have gained immense popularity in recent years, offering a fun and interactive way for users to engage with their audience and generate buzz around their brand. For real estate agents, participating in or creating social media challenges can help to humanize your brand, showcase your personality, and connect with potential clients in a more personal and authentic way. In this chapter, we will explore how to effectively participate in and create social media challenges that resonate with your target audience and support your overall marketing goals.

Understanding Social Media Challenges:

Social media challenges are activities or tasks that users complete and share on their social media platforms, often using a specific hashtag to connect with others participating in the same challenge. These challenges can range from simple, lighthearted fun to more meaningful campaigns that support a cause or raise awareness around an issue.

Some popular examples of social media challenges include the Ice Bucket Challenge, the Mannequin Challenge, and the Dance Challenge.

Benefits of Participating in Social Media Challenges:

Participating in social media challenges can offer several benefits to real estate agents, including:

- Increased engagement: Challenges encourage users to interact with your content, boosting your overall engagement metrics.
- Greater visibility: Using popular challenge hashtags can help to increase the visibility of your content and attract new followers.
- Enhanced brand personality: Challenges allow you to showcase your personality, making your brand more relatable and approachable.
- Networking opportunities: Connecting with other users participating in the same challenge can help to expand your professional network.

Tips for Participating in Social Media Challenges:

When participating in social media challenges, consider the following tips to ensure a successful outcome:

- Choose challenges that align with your brand: Select challenges that are relevant to your target audience and support your overall brand messaging.

- Be authentic: Participate in challenges that genuinely interest you and showcase your personality in a genuine manner.
- Encourage engagement: Invite your audience to participate in the challenge with you, share their experiences, and use the challenge hashtag.
- Stay on top of trends: Monitor social media platforms to stay informed about trending challenges and identify potential opportunities for participation.

Creating Your Own Social Media Challenge:

In addition to participating in existing challenges, real estate agents can also create their own social media challenges to generate buzz around their brand and engage their audience. Here are some steps to follow when creating a social media challenge:

- Define your objective: Determine the goal of your challenge, whether it's to increase brand awareness, generate leads, or drive website traffic.
- Develop a unique concept: Brainstorm ideas for your challenge that are relevant to your target audience and resonate with their interests.
- Create a hashtag: Develop a unique and memorable hashtag for your challenge to track engagement and encourage users to participate.
- Promote your challenge: Share your challenge on all your social media platforms, encouraging your followers to participate and share their experiences using the challenge hashtag.

- Engage with participants: Monitor the challenge hashtag and engage with users who participate in your challenge, offering encouragement and support.

Social media challenges present a unique opportunity for real estate agents to engage with their audience and showcase their personality in a fun and interactive manner. By participating in existing challenges and creating your own, you can effectively humanize your brand, increase visibility, and connect with potential clients on a deeper level.

CHAPTER 75:

SOCIAL MEDIA SCAVENGER HUNT

A social media scavenger hunt is an interactive, engaging, and entertaining way to promote your real estate business, connect with your target audience, and generate buzz around your brand. By leveraging social media platforms and the power of user-generated content, a well-executed scavenger hunt can help to increase brand awareness, drive website traffic, and even generate leads for your business. In this chapter, we will discuss how to plan, execute, and promote a social media scavenger hunt that delivers meaningful results for your real estate business.

Planning Your Social Media Scavenger Hunt:

Before you launch your scavenger hunt, it's essential to develop a clear plan that outlines your objectives, target audience, and overall strategy. Some key elements to consider during the planning stage include:

- Objectives: Define the primary goals of your scavenger hunt, such as increasing brand awareness, driving website traffic, or generating leads.
- Target audience: Identify the demographic and psychographic characteristics of your ideal participants, ensuring your scavenger hunt is relevant and appealing to them.
- Platforms: Choose the social media platforms that best align with your target audience and overall marketing objectives.
- Duration: Determine the length of your scavenger hunt, keeping in mind that shorter, more focused hunts may generate greater engagement.

Creating the Scavenger Hunt:

Once you have a clear plan in place, it's time to create the scavenger hunt itself. Some key elements to include in your scavenger hunt are:

- Challenges: Develop a series of challenges or tasks for participants to complete throughout the scavenger hunt. These challenges should be relevant to your target audience, showcase your local community, and highlight your real estate expertise.
- Clues: Create clues or hints that guide participants through the scavenger hunt, encouraging them to explore your local area and engage with your content.

- Hashtags: Develop a unique and memorable hashtag for your scavenger hunt to track engagement, encourage participation, and facilitate conversation among participants.
- Prizes: Offer a prize or incentive for participants who successfully complete the scavenger hunt, such as a gift card, discount on your services, or branded merchandise.

Promoting Your Social Media Scavenger Hunt:

With your scavenger hunt created, it's time to promote the event and generate interest among your target audience. Consider using the following strategies to promote your scavenger hunt:

- Announce the event on your social media channels, using the scavenger hunt hashtag and eye-catching visuals to capture attention.
- Create a dedicated landing page on your website that provides details about the scavenger hunt, including instructions, rules, and a registration form.
- Share teaser content leading up to the event, such as behind-the-scenes sneak peeks or hints about the challenges participants will face.
- Partner with local businesses, influencers, or community organizations to help promote the event and encourage participation.

Engaging with Participants:

Throughout the scavenger hunt, it's essential to engage with participants and monitor their progress. Consider the following strategies to maintain engagement:

- Respond to comments, questions, and messages from participants in a timely manner, offering support and encouragement as needed.
- Share user-generated content from participants on your own social media channels, celebrating their progress and showcasing the fun and excitement of the event.
- Offer real-time updates and leaderboards to foster a sense of competition and camaraderie among participants.
- Announce the winners and celebrate their accomplishments at the end of the event, thanking all participants for their involvement.

A social media scavenger hunt offers an engaging and interactive way for real estate agents to connect with their target audience, showcase their local expertise, and generate buzz around their brand. By carefully planning, executing, and promoting your scavenger hunt, you can create a memorable event that delivers meaningful results for your real estate business. Remember to keep your target audience in mind throughout the entire process, ensuring that your scavenger hunt is relevant, engaging, and enjoyable for all participants. With the right strategy and commitment, a social media scavenger hunt can be a valuable addition to your overall marketing efforts, helping you to stand out from the competition and build lasting relationships with your clients and community.

CHAPTER 76:

30 DAY SOCIAL MEDIA PLAN

A well-structured and consistent social media plan is essential for any real estate agent looking to expand their online presence and generate leads. A 30-day social media plan can be a powerful tool for boosting engagement, increasing brand awareness, and attracting potential clients. In this chapter, we'll outline a comprehensive 30-day social media plan for real estate agents, with step-by-step guidance on creating and scheduling content, monitoring engagement, and evaluating success.

Week 1: Setting the Foundation

- Define your goals: Start by setting clear and measurable goals for your social media efforts. These could include increasing brand awareness, generating leads, or driving traffic to your website.
- Identify your target audience: Understand who your ideal clients are and tailor your content to meet their needs and interests.

- Audit your current social media presence: Review your existing social media profiles and identify areas for improvement. Ensure your profiles are complete, accurate, and consistent across platforms.
- Create a content calendar: Plan and schedule your content for the next 30 days. Make sure to include a mix of promotional, educational, and engaging content that appeals to your target audience.

Week 2: Creating and Curating Content

- Develop original content: Create blog posts, videos, images, and other content that showcases your expertise and highlights your personality.
- Curate relevant content: Share articles, news, and resources from industry experts and local sources that your audience will find valuable.
- Leverage user-generated content: Encourage clients and followers to share their experiences, testimonials, and photos with you. Repost and credit their content to showcase your successful partnerships.
- Experiment with different content formats: Test various content types, such as live videos, stories, and carousel posts, to determine which resonate best with your audience.

Week 3: Engaging with Your Audience

- Respond to comments and messages: Be proactive in acknowledging and answering inquiries from your audience to foster relationships and trust.

- Engage with other profiles: Like, comment, and share content from other local businesses, industry influencers, and potential clients to expand your network and increase visibility.
- Monitor your competitors: Keep an eye on what your competitors are doing on social media and learn from their successes and failures.
- Host a live Q&A session: Use live video to answer questions from your audience and showcase your expertise in real-time.

Week 4: Tracking and Optimizing Your Strategy

- Analyze your metrics: Review your social media analytics to track your progress towards your goals and identify patterns in engagement.
- Adjust your content strategy: Based on your analytics, refine your content plan to focus on the most successful content types and topics.
- Experiment with post timing: Test posting at different times of day and days of the week to determine when your audience is most active and engaged.
- Evaluate your advertising efforts: Review the performance of your social media ads and adjust your targeting, budget, and creative as needed to maximize results.

CHAPTER 77:

SOCIAL MEDIA AUDIT

A social media audit is a comprehensive review of your social media presence to assess its effectiveness and identify areas for improvement. It helps real estate agents ensure their profiles are optimized, consistent, and aligned with their goals. In this chapter, we'll outline the steps to conduct a social media audit and provide actionable insights for refining your social media strategy.

Step 1: Make a List of Your Social Media Accounts

Start by listing all your social media accounts, including both personal and professional profiles. Don't forget any accounts that you may have created but no longer actively use. This step will give you a clear overview of your entire online presence.

Step 2: Evaluate Your Profiles

Go through each profile and examine the following elements:

- Profile picture and cover photo: Ensure your images are high-quality, professional, and consistent across platforms.
- Bio and description: Check that your bio is up-to-date, highlights your expertise, and includes relevant keywords and contact information.
- Username and URL: Verify that your username and URL are consistent and easily identifiable across all platforms.
- Posting frequency: Assess whether you are posting consistently and at a frequency that aligns with best practices for each platform.

Step 3: Analyze Your Content

Review the content you've shared over the past few months and evaluate the following aspects:
- Content mix: Determine if you have a good balance of promotional, educational, and engaging content.
- Post format: Check if you are utilizing a variety of post formats (e.g., images, videos, links) and leveraging platform-specific features (e.g., Stories, Reels, Live).
- Engagement: Identify which types of content generate the most likes, comments, and shares, and consider how you can create more of this content.
- Branding: Ensure your content aligns with your brand voice, visual identity, and overall messaging.

Step 4: Assess Your Engagement

Take a closer look at your interactions with your audience:

- Response time: Measure how quickly you respond to comments and messages from your followers.
- Follower growth: Monitor your follower growth rate and identify any trends or fluctuations.
- Audience demographics: Review the demographics of your audience to ensure you are reaching your target market.

Step 5: Analyze Your Competitors

Review the social media profiles of your competitors to gain insights into their strategies and identify areas where you can differentiate yourself:

- Content types: Observe the types of content your competitors are sharing and assess their engagement levels.
- Posting frequency: Compare your posting frequency with your competitors and note any differences.
- Engagement strategies: Identify the tactics your competitors use to engage with their audience and consider how you can adopt or improve upon these strategies.

Step 6: Develop an Action Plan

Based on your audit findings, create an action plan to improve your social media presence:

- Optimize profiles: Update your profile information, images, and URLs as needed.
- Adjust content strategy: Refine your content mix, post formats, and posting frequency based on your analysis.

- Improve engagement: Implement new engagement strategies and prioritize responding to comments and messages.
- Monitor progress: Continuously track your social media performance and adjust your action plan as needed.

A social media audit is a valuable exercise for real estate agents to ensure their online presence is optimized and effective. By conducting regular audits, you can identify areas for improvement, better understand your audience, and ultimately, strengthen your social media strategy for increased success.

CONCLUSION

As we reach the end of this comprehensive guide to social media marketing for real estate agents, it's important to reflect on the valuable insights and actionable strategies you've gained throughout this journey. Social media is a powerful tool that, when used effectively, can help you grow your real estate business, build strong relationships with clients, and establish yourself as an industry leader.

In this book, we've explored various social media platforms, including Facebook, YouTube, Instagram, Pinterest, and TikTok, and provided practical tips and strategies for optimizing your presence on each platform. From setting up professional profiles and creating engaging content to leveraging advertising options and cross-promoting your efforts, you now have the knowledge and tools to succeed in the ever-evolving world of social media.

We've also delved into the importance of understanding your target audience, crafting a unique brand voice, and developing a consistent visual identity. By focusing on these elements, you can create a cohesive and memorable online presence that resonates with your audience and sets you apart from your competition.

Additionally, this guide has provided resources for managing your online reputation, staying motivated, and overcoming common challenges, as well as practical tips for using graphic design, stock image, and video editing tools to enhance your content.

As you continue to refine your social media strategy, remember that success takes time, effort, and persistence. Be prepared to adapt to new trends and emerging platforms, and always strive to learn from your experiences and data. Regularly evaluate your performance through social media audits and analytics to ensure you're making informed decisions and optimizing your efforts for the best possible results.

In closing, we hope that this book has provided you with the knowledge, inspiration, and confidence to take your real estate business to new heights through the power of social media marketing. As you embark on this exciting journey, remember to stay true to your unique brand, engage meaningfully with your audience, and always strive to deliver exceptional value. The sky's the limit, and we can't wait to see your success unfold.

HAPPY SELLING!

Printed in Great Britain
by Amazon

45963169R00198